ARTHUR

Thank You for Being Jesus' Love

Sr. Ave Clark, O.P.
<u>**Heart to Heart Ministry**</u>
718-428-2471
Pearlbud7@aol.com

<u>**Rachel Prayer Hour**</u>:   post abortion syndrome
<u>**Elizabeth Ministry**</u>: for parents who lost a child
<u>**Caring Hearts**</u>: for people with PTSD
<u>**Samaritan Hearts**</u>: for victims of tragic crimes
<u>**SOS**</u>:   for survivors of suicide
<u>**Roses**</u>: for survivors of abuse/violence/domestic violence
<u>**ACOA**</u>: for Adult Children of Alcoholics
<u>**Caritas:**</u> for family with children and adults with disability
<u>**Hearts Afire**</u>: domestic violence sessions (individual)
<u>**Lights in the Darkness**</u>: for persons seeking healing from
                                        depression
<u>**Bereavement Sessions**</u>: From the Heart (individual)
<u>**Spiritual Direction**</u>: Open your Heart (Individual)
<u>**Pastoral Prayerline**</u>: A Listening Heart
<u>**Heart to Heart Prayer Chats**</u>: Across the Country

Only the wings of Love and Compassion
can lift and carry us….

ARTHUR

Thank You for Being Jesus' Love

Sr. Ave Clark, O.P.

CONTENTS

Dedication

This book is dedicated to all people with
special needs
who teach us to always hope and to persevere,
to believe in one's innate goodness
and to celebrate the sacred gift of life
in all its' dignity and humanity.

"Be who you were created to be
and you will set the world on fire."
(St. Catherine of Sienna)

PROLOGUE

THE GREATEST RESURRECTION GIFT
(article written for the Tablet, Brooklyn, NY Diocese
two months after Arthur passed away)

What a beautiful season Easter is – a time to sing joyously, Alleluia, Alleluia! But I've been singing with some tears this Easter season for my dear friend Arthur.

Arthur and I have known each other over 10 years. Arthur would call me every day, sometimes five to seven times a day just to share about his love for Jesus.

A convert to the faith, Arthur became a Catholic at St. Jude Church in Canarsie, where the community welcomed him with great respect and caring. He told me that becoming a Catholic made his heart forever happy. St. Jude's parish would be his forever family.

Arthur moved a few years ago to Belle Harbor, and joined St. Francis de Sales parish where he continued to attend Mass.

He would tell me just what the priest would say in his homily. He especially liked Father Jim Cunningham's sharings.

Arthur told me about the prayer garden at the parish where he liked to stop and reflect on Jesus' goodness in his life.

LEANING ON JESUS

Holy Saturday, I picked Arthur up at the Belle Harbor Manor for people with mental illness. Arthur had schizophrenia, which he bore courageously. He would say to me: "I lean on Jesus' love to help me".

We went to St. Francis de Sales Church for a visit. I lit a candle for Arthur. He smiled and thanked me for doing that. We prayed 10 Hail Mary's together. After that, we went to the prayer garden and sat together, reflecting quietly.

Then I noticed his shoelaces were untied. I leaned over quietly to tie them. As I looked up,
Arthur was smiling and said, "Thank you, Sister, for being Jesus' love for me. "

I smiled feeling humbled by his kind and holy words.

We went to Dunkin' Donuts, his favorite place, and then as I drove him back to Belle Harbor Manor, he told me to have a nice time with my family and to tell them he said hello. He said he would pray for them on Easter.

Then I thanked him for being Jesus' love for me. I gave Arthur a bag of goodies and a gift card for Dunkin' Donuts. He said he would share the gifts with others. I also gave him a prayer shawl someone made. I told him to put it on his bed; it would be like Jesus was wrapping His arms around Arthur.

Before he left the car, I gave him a hug and said, "Arthur, God bless you always". He smiled.

He called me that evening and said he had the prayer shawl around him. We both agreed we had a wonderful Holy Saturday.

When I got home Easter evening from visiting my family in New Jersey, I had a few messages on my answering machine. I smiled when I heard them.

On Easter Monday, I went to get my mail and found a special card for me from Arthur: Wishes for a Joyous Easter NUN on this joyous day. And I thought to myself, I am blessed to have Arthur as a dear friend.

A few hours later, I received a telephone call that Arthur had passed away Easter evening.

My dear friend Arthur had the greatest resurrection gift this Easter season. He is seeing Jesus face to face and I can imagine Arthur saying, "Lord, thank you for all the love you shared with me on earth".

Arthur, Alleluia, Alleluia! You are risen in glory now!

Yes, I have tears of missing you and your calls, but I also have a wonderful smile, Arthur, for your gift of prayer, which you shared with me and so many others.

You gave me blessings galore – sincerity, humility, simplicity, forgiveness, kindness, charity and a sense of humor – that I will treasure forever. Most of all Arthur you gave me an extraordinary example of Faith-lived. Alleluia He is Risen!

(The Tablet – Brooklyn Diocese, June 2017)

Author's Note

I have written this book in memory of my wonderful and special friend named Arthur Mirell. In my writing, I wanted to share how Arthur lived his life with such love and caring. I also hope that in your reading the stories about Arthur you will find a deeper appreciation for what it means to be a person of goodness.

Very early in life, Arthur was diagnosed with a mental illness called schizophrenia. With his gentle nature Arthur would get up every day and set out to live his life well even amidst difficulties and struggles. He was very aware of his struggles and at times shared with me how weary he was feeling. However, he chose to define his life not by his limitations but rather by his wonderful Faith life that would be for Arthur a beautiful light of hope that he would share with others.

One special gift Arthur shared with me was how he was so appreciative, ever so grateful for any act of kindness extended to him: a simple gesture of welcome, a car ride home, a gift card to Dunkin Donuts, or a phone call chat...all received with his graciousness of spirit and his sincere words saying, "Thank you for being Jesus' love for me."

Arthur's example of living a life of love and kindness would become for me a wonderful light of Jesus' presence. I hope as you read this book you will feel that you now know Arthur and will discover in his humble words, deeds, and actions graces for your life journey.

"To know Arthur is to know Jesus' Love"
(Sister Ave Clark, O.P)

"For God made
His light to shine
in our Hearts."
(2 Cor. 4:6)

Another King Arthur

I never met Arthur
But that is not to say I do not know him
I have never met Jesus
Yet I believe I know Him

I was in the chapel of a convent in the church of Queens
Where we gather to pray and sing and listen
It was there and then when I learned of the life of Arthur

Like Jesus, Arthur carried a cross
We all do
Arthur's was in his mind
At times it betrayed, denied, and abandoned him
But it did not defeat him
Arthur's kind and humble spirit was just too strong
He faced his suffering with quiet faith and noble dignity
Arthur's loving and giving nature touched those around him

So also like Jesus, Arthur was a kind of king
Lord of the realm of simple humility
Hail Arthur, king of gratitude and grace

We could all learn from him
We should all live in such a place

by James Palermo

(James Palermo, a gifted poet with heart words written in prose. He himself is disabled with blindness and sees the world through his faith-lived)

James Palermo, who wrote the poem, "Another King Arthur" was at a retreat I gave when I shared about Arthur's life. James told me that he was a poet. "Oh", I said, "would you write a poem about my friend Arthur?" The poem certainly expressed quite simply who Arthur was and I can only imagine Arthur's humble smile at being called a "King".

What a beautiful gift my friend Arthur lived…a life so noble of spirit, always grateful, full of grace…a life defined by loving one another as Jesus loved us. For many years, I have ministered to/with people with disabilities (special needs). So often, it was I who learned to see life anew in a creative way. Years ago, I taught special education classes…I realized all too soon (a blessing for me) that my students with special needs taught **me** about life and how to live life:

-to be brave
-to be forgiving
-to accept limitations
-to never make fun of anyone
-to have a sense of humor
-to open my heart with great compassion
-to be understanding
-to be very patient
-to recognize my own humanity

-to be faithful…no matter what!!

Once I told Arthur that he was a great teacher. "How is that?" he asked. I said, "Well, Arthur, when I sometimes suggest something to you that I think will help, you listen very patiently and thank me for my caring suggestion and say now that just may work. I remember in one conversation you were sad that some people made fun of you at your assigned table for supper. I thought if you spoke to the social workers they might be able to work out a new table or deal with the people not being so kind. I remember thinking to myself that would be the best way to handle this upsetment." You listened and then thanked me for the suggestion, but you decided to do something else. "Gulp", I thought, "what would that be?" "Oh", Arthur said very kindly, "I will just turn in a different direction." In other words, turn his cheek…not strike back with harsher words.

"Oh, Arthur…you are right – thank you for teaching me to do the right thing…to be a peace giver by my attitude." Days later he said, "it worked", and I smiled thinking, "thank you Arthur, for being Jesus' love for me." Now you all know why Arthur **is** a King…a King of loving every day.

Arthur's love, even for others who at times made fun of him, will always be an example to me and to others who read this book:

> --not to return unkind words
> --not to berate differences
> --not to hate or inflict harm

By his attitude of sincere forgiveness, Arthur showed us the courage we can all have...to turn the other way – a better way of non-violence – a way of heart peace.

Cards

You usually go to a stationary store to find cards for a special occasion or one that just says, "I care". You wander up and down each aisle, reading the inside of each card then choose just the right one for the person for whom you are buying the card...you get home...write a few extra words...then send it on its way. You get a good feeling of inner peace and happiness thinking of the receiver of the card. A few days later... a call comes...the voice, filled with joy or comfort, expresses how much the card meant. Ahh how happy you are to have found that card!

Basically, it is more than the card that made your recipient feel so happy or consoled. It was the thought and time you put into finding that very special card. In fact, you probably could have written what you wanted on a plain piece of paper; but, it was the extra touch of caring that warmed another human heart...heart-to-heart for sure.

Over the years, I have received beautiful cards from Arthur. One time he told me he was going out and would call me later. After about six hours he called and told me he had a wonderful day. He said he had taken about seven buses to different stores and was so happy that he finally found what he was looking for. I asked what that was and he told me <u>two cards</u>. It was Christmas time and there was snow and ice on the ground. He went all over Brooklyn, on and off buses just for two cards!! He said one was for me and one was for Sister Mary at St. Jude's. I smiled and said I am looking forward to receiving mine in the mail. Four days later the card came, "Merry Christmas to a Nun". Arthur didn't just pick any card in a store; he traveled on many buses to many stores until he found just the right card. How Sister Mary and I treasured those cards!

The last card I received from Arthur was for Easter, which arrived on Easter Monday, 2017. He told me I might get the card after Easter since he only mailed it on Thursday of Holy Week. I told him I'd love it even more to receive it after Easter — "it really means you cared to send it to me". He said, "I sure do".

I opened the card and smiled -- Pink tulips and the printed message "Easter Wish for A Wonderful Nun on this Joyous Holiday". Arthur added his own words to the card written in a circle. (He said he writes in circles because the world is round.) So I read Arthur's words as I turned the card in a circle. His ending words I will cherish forever..."You as an O.P. (Order of Preachers-Dominican) are made by Christ and molded as an angel for me...". I sat quietly with tears and great happiness thinking of how Arthur somehow finds these special cards. Then the phone rang...I was told Arthur passed away early in the morning. It was Easter time and I had a beautiful card from Arthur.

Candles On The Cake

As the years go by all too quickly, most of us only want a few candles on our birthday cake. Why is that? Do we not want to embrace each year of that aging process of life? Last year, I invited Arthur and his friends from St. Jude's Parish to come to my residence for a party to celebrate his 70th birthday. Everyone was so excited to bring something to add to the party and of course a gift for Arthur. When I told Arthur of these plans, he was extremely happy and with his "as always" sincere words said, "I can't thank you enough for celebrating my life."

We gathered around the table with lively conversation and Arthur telling us stories of how happy he was to have such good friends. Tears were in everyone's eyes as they said a prayer for Arthur and thanked him for being such an inspiring and faithful friend. Then he opened his gifts ~~ "Oh, a Dunkin Donuts card; Oh my, a gift card to McDonalds, I shall enjoy myself." Arthur read each card and acknowledged the person who gave the gift with very sincere and heart-warming words:

"Thank you for being a good friend"

"Thank you for sharing your time with me"

"Thank you for your good prayers"

"Thank you for welcoming me into your heart"

"Thank you for the 7 candles on the cake

$$10 \times 7 = 70"$$

We all laughed and then Arthur said, "thank you for being Jesus' love for me". In silence, we shed tears of great joy for celebrating Arthur's life. The cake was brought in with 7 candles...$10 \times 7 = 70$...and we all sang 'Happy Birthday dear Arthur'. He blew out the candles and said, "I wish you all Peace and Happiness." The **gift** was Arthur. In receiving, Arthur shared friendship and acceptance, joy and understanding. Arthur would also give to each one of us at the celebration of his life 10 x 7 = 70 feelings of what it means to be a friend, a Christian, a neighbor, a sister, and a brother to each other.

What does it mean to be a person so full of humanity with limitations, struggles, and even heartaches? To me, Arthur shows us by his every breath, every footstep, and every act of charity…that humanity is not defined by limitations but rather by how we each choose to **live** life and love one another.

Many of Arthur's 70 years were spent in severe mental suffering…he courageously embraced his disability as part of his human condition. But Arthur was more than his struggles…he was pure goodness. Our world needs more of what Arthur was.

Arthur's example and goodness will live on. I know his goodness is a gift for my life and hopefully for all those who will read and reflect on Arthur's words of simplicity, charity and kindness. Little did any of us know that Arthur's 70th birthday party would be his last on earth. It will always be a reminder to me of how wonderful a gift it is to see candles on the cake… whatever our age.

A Rich Man

Arthur was a rich man...not in worldly wealth, degrees or property owned. No, he was rich in being a person of virtues and values lived.   If someone would ask me to describe Arthur I would stop only for a moment and smile as I would describe him as a good man, a just man, a fine gentleman, a wonderful friend, a caring heart, a forgiving soul and above all a man who sowed peace in our world.

Arthur's way of living and being was grounded in the daily breath of his compassionate heart. He felt deeply for people suffering in any way. One day he shared with me how he offered to go to AA meetings with one of his friends who was very addicted to alcohol. Arthur did not judge his friend; he offered to be his companion on the journey.

When his friend passed away, Arthur spoke so kindly about him saying he struggled bravely carrying his cross; and Arthur was proud to help him carry it. Arthur was rich in acknowledging the small steps of courage others took to gain wholeness and healing. He understood that his own small steps of dealing with the severe effects of schizophrenia had given him a heart that shared the presence of love…a love like Jesus that endured…even death on the cross.

One of Arthur's richest gifts is what I would call "radical kindness". On one of his visits to my home Arthur noticed a plaque on the wall that said 'Keep it simple…Love Everyone'. He smiled and said, "I like the meaning of the plaque's saying". We both sat quietly, then I asked him if it is really possible to love everyone. He replied, "Well at least we can try." In other words, we might not always feel like loving everybody or we might wonder how we can love people who inflict harm on others. Where do we get the grace to lay down our swords of harsh words, cruel deeds, and gossip chatter? We can always try.

Arthur did that every day. He never gave up being a peace giver.

Arthur told me at times he felt the loneliness and exclusion his disease bestowed upon him. No one wants to feel lonely, left out, ignored or rejected for being a human being with a disease of the mind. My 'rich in spirit' friend felt the poverty of the world. He said when he had these feelings he would go to the prayer garden at his church and sit quietly, not stewing in anger or hurt but just resting in the comfort of God's creation. Arthur put the face of love...Jesus' love into his heart. He was truly a rich man...rich in peacefulness of spirit. Thank you, Arthur, for sharing your richness with so many.

Blessed Margaret of Castello

"Although You have hidden these things
from the wise and the learned,
You have revealed them to little ones."
(Matthew 11:25)

I am a Dominican sister and one of my favorite Dominicans is a very hidden "blessed" person. Her name is Blessed Margaret of Castello. She was born a midget who was blind, hunchback, lame and ugly. She was scorned and abandoned early in life. Her story could make us angry at peoples' rejection of one so disabled and in need. But instead, her story is one of the resilience of the human spirit and also of a loving heart that looked beyond the painful injustices heaped upon her. Margaret kept a charitable heart even concerning those who should have loved her.

Margaret became a "Mantellate" (lay Dominican) living with different families who kindly took her in. She was a prayerful woman who was led by the

Spirit to help those in need. She visited people in prisons and those who hungered for physical and spiritual food. Margaret brought fresh hope and courage to hundreds of weary souls. Her story has been retold through the centuries and it continues to inspire hope to anyone who has felt discouraged by adversities or feelings that life was not worth living.

I gave Arthur a book about Blessed Margaret of Castello. He told me that when he quietly and slowly read it, he felt that Blessed Margaret was talking to him about how to love Jesus with unshakeable faith. This was Arthur's faith…always loving, caring about others, never holding a grudge, accepting his disability with the crosses it brought. Like Margaret, Arthur befriended people who were suffering, not out of pity but with great compassion.

I see in Blessed Margaret and Arthur a beautiful reflection of Jesus' simplicity of spirit. Both of them lived their lives completely dependent on Divine love. They are the "little ones" who recognize Jesus' love in everyone and in all the circumstances of life. I imagine my friend Arthur meeting Blessed Margaret in heaven. After introducing himself he would tell her he had a Dominican sister friend on earth who coordinated Heart to Heart Ministry. I see her smiling and saying to Arthur, "you have lived your life with such charity. May your life continue to reach out, heart to heart, to a world so in need of your 'blessed' intercessions." I also imagine Blessed Margaret and Arthur looking at each other with a smile...a smile knowing that their very soul-spirit was never disabled...it truly lived in glory, here on earth, in hearts that touched so many with kind gestures, peace-filled words and deeds and above all with unshakeable Faith.

The Positive Side of Life

"Keep your face always toward the sunshine and the shadows will fall behind you."

(Walt Whitman)

Living with a mental illness takes extraordinary energy every day. I had read this sentence and quoted it to Arthur and asked him where he got his extraordinary energy. "Well", Arthur said, "I don't always feel I have the physical or emotional energy as I get quite weary with my illness journey". Then he asked, "Have you ever felt weary?" "Ahh, yes I have Arthur." "What kept you going?" he asked. (Both of us asked each other the same questions. We wanted to know how we could help each other.)

There was a time I told him in my life that the shadow of depression and anxiety overwhelmed me and even the ordinary daily chores of life weighed heavily. What helped me (still does) was the inner courage to take small steps toward the sunshine of life and believe what someone once told me: "You are valiant, your spirit though struggling and stumbling will arise." That's the positive side to believe in ~~ Arise!

Arthur listened intently. He told me he loved the days when he felt the sunshine was in his spirit and when he felt the clouds hiding his sunshine he would not give up. He leaned on the hearts of others' caring. His 6, 7, and sometimes 8 calls a day told me that Arthur was leaning on the heart of Jesus' love that I offered to him. This humbled me but it also made me realize that Arthur and I were pilgrim souls journeying to wholeness. I think what kept Arthur and myself going was this quiet inner light of hope that we shared with each other. This is the hope that sees the inner side of positive thinking, of seeing a sunset beyond the clouds and the rain or the thunder bolts of life's journey. This hope lifts a candle in the darkness of any struggling moment.

I gave Arthur a small tea light and batteries. He told me he put it on in the morning to thank God for the day and at night he put it on again to thank the Lord for the night sky of stars. The small light made him feel safe and happy. It was like Jesus being right there with him every step of the way. Jesus reminds us: "Do not be afraid, I am with you." Arthur believed this. I gave him not just a light but an assurance of my support and great caring that deepened his belief that he could have life-goals, dreams and above all good friendships. Isn't that what life is all about~~sharing hope and being a positive force in life?

Arthur loved life. He always had something positive to share about the weather, the food, a change in schedule, the program he went to, the people he met, his roommate, his visits to church, his phone conversations and above all his love of God.

He always had something positive to do or be: show compassion for people suffering, forgive slights, understand other's loss, laugh at simple jokes, attend Mass and after Mass social get-togethers, smile as you share a cup of coffee, and send cards of gratitude to those who share Jesus' love with you. What a list! I would say that Arthur lived on the positive side of life. He viewed life with a spark of hope. Arthur, you are now a bright star <u>shining</u> <u>forever</u> in the heavens.

Humility

Let's look at **humility** as a wonderful, wholesome gift. To be grounded, to appreciate the very essence of life is to be humble of heart, soul and spirit. Humility is not self-effacing; rather, it is to acknowledge what we have, do not have, who we are and are becoming as a noble unfolding of life.

Humility lets us give to others and lets us ask when we are needy. It rejoices with joy and comforts any sorrow. It respects diversity and understands limitations. Humility graces all of life with hope.

Humility enhances life, it does not diminish life. It is always thoughtful, embraces struggles and hardships, rejoices in small and ordinary joys and successes. Humility does not discount anyone. It does not ignore injustices. It does not speak harshly or irreverently. Humility is like the sunflower seeking out the light in darkness, sorrow, tragedy, loss, dis-appointment, or sense of abandonment in our every-day ordinary tears.

Humility is the foundation of a noble spirit. It is born in every human heart. Let us believe this!

I write these words and know that I am very often comforted and challenged by humility not to walk away from the humble way, but believe that we can inspire one another to grow noble in spirit as each one of us dares to embrace a life of wonderful humili-ty.

I have neighbors next door who work so hard to grow a garden of fruits and vegetables. They begin every Spring and by Summertime they are holding up their ripened crops. I so enjoy watching their humble joy. I also enjoy finding squash, string beans, carrots and zucchini left at my door with a note, "enjoy our great vegetables", signed your good neighbors.

This note and announcement of green and good is not bragging~~it is truly a sign of sharing joyful humility. It lifts one up, helps a spirit to soar and adds to the gift of being a grateful noble soul.

My good neighbors toiled long hours on their knees planting, weeding, watering and sheltering the garden through storms and dry spaces. To reap the fruit and vegetables of the garden of life one must share with humble service and sacrifices and weeding what doesn't work and wait humbly for the seeds to take root and bloom and then humbly rejoice and share life. To be humble is to be holy.

I made a bag of goodies for Arthur ~~ a vegetable salad from my neighbors' garden of gifts. Arthur told me it was delicious and to tell my neighbors thanks for sharing their garden of joy with him.

He went on to say~~that to appreciate their kindness was a sign of humility…a humble thanks for all that we have and can share.

"Humility is saying thanks" and being a vessel of God's love. Thank you, Arthur, for being a humble steward of Jesus' love.

Just What Is Greatness?!

I love Mary's Magnificat~~

> "He has put down the mighty from their thrones
> and has lifted up the lowly..." (Luke 1:52)

Perhaps what we are hearing anew in this prayer is the beautiful blessing of being lifted up. This usually is done because of trusting, hoping and wanting to be one with the Lord. To be lifted up...is to get up because of Jesus' love by sharing an affirmation, an encouraging word, caring support, a whispered prayer and a faithful heart.

All of these qualities, virtues and kind acts empower the lowly ones of which we all are at some time in our life. This becomes a holy awareness moment to believe in and embrace our own humanity and see in our struggles and crucifixion moments of dying to self as a new resurrection~~our very selves evolving and becoming the Word of Jesus loved and lived with grace~~this is the greatness of holiness.

This is the best way to live in an interior way...**all for Jesus**. It is also the best way to live in our exterior demeanor and actions...to be for others, not controlling, manipulating or in oppressive ways. The greatness of life resides in a giving spirit, one that is freeing and all embracing. This is being Jesus' love here on earth.

Arthur would tell me people would ask him for money sometimes promising to pay him back. Some never did and others would pay him only some of what he had loaned them. Very often I would gently suggest to Arthur to be careful about lending money, especially to those who would take advantage of Arthur's good nature. Arthur told me that he knew when he lent money that some people would never pay him back. He then would tell me it is better to give generously and that his money wasn't going to bring him happiness if he selfishly guarded it.

One day a man who owed Arthur $31 gave him $9 in return payment. Arthur thanked the man for the payment and never mentioned that the man still owed him $22. The man looked at Arthur and said, "the Lord lives in you Arthur." That is for sure! I will always be inspired by Arthur's greatness of spirit. I hope you will too.

With so little, Arthur shared so much...his abundance was not in money but in his respectful and generous heart~~a heart lifted up by Divine Love. Thank you, Arthur, for being a blessing of greatness...giving...giving...giving... always rooted in Jesus' love.

Pope Francis and Arthur

"Mercy unites us to respond to life

with love, compassion,

forgiveness and generosity

within our families, our neighborhoods

our nation and world.

As we have experienced

God's unlimited mercy,

so must we choose

to give it to others.

Mercy can transform us

and bring true peace

to our world"

(Pope Francis)

"Mercy is in my eyes,

my hands and

most of all in my heart."

(Arthur Mirell)

Arthur loved reading about Pope Francis especially in Father Robert Lauder's books, <u>Pope Francis Spirituality and Our Story</u> and <u>Pope Francis Profound Personalism and Poverty.</u> Arthur liked Father Lauder's sharing of mercy as "God's Yes". Every day Arthur was God's Yes of mercy.

Arthur lived 1Cor 13:4-8 – "Love is patient, kind, not jealous or rude, never pompous or inflated, not seeking our own interests; not quick tempered, not brooding over injuries, never rejoicing over a wrong doing, but rejoicing in the truth – bears all things, believes all things, endures all things and loves with a love that never fails."

This is the love Pope Francis encourages us to live, promote and inspire by example. It is a love that carries the cross that resurrects time and time again. It is a love that is born of humility and suffering. It is a quiet and often hidden love. It is a love with an all-embracing light that welcomes all.

Just like Pope Francis, Arthur set out in life with his beautiful heart of mercy – a heart of great compassion that knew rejection, mocking and crucifixion of spirit – but Arthur in his poverty of spirit did something wonderful with his worn shoes with holes, his plaid shirt with stains and his fragmented mental state on difficult days.

Arthur trusted and believed Jesus was walking with him, resting with him, and sometimes weeping with him. Arthur believed Jesus' mercy wrapped Arthur in peace, joy, hope, courage, compassion, and above all friendship.

Arthur told me the more he read what Pope Francis said, the more he knew Jesus love. We all know how the Pope speaks, especially through his actions. One thing Pope Francis said that helped Arthur to smile was "Christian life is bearing witness with cheerfulness as Jesus did." Arthur said, "Sister, it only costs a grin to smile like Jesus."

One day Arthur and I stopped by the prayer garden at Sacred Heart of Jesus Church where there is a beautiful Celtic Irish Cross. Arthur said to me "you must like that cross a lot!" Boy did I have an Irish grin of joy on my face that day! We looked at the prayer bricks on the garden path. Arthur smiled when I showed him the one I donated for Heart to Heart Ministry.

I asked Arthur if he would like to have a brick. He said "Yes, what does it cost?" I replied, "Just being Jesus' love." We talked about what he would like engraved on it. I suggested his name, Arthur Mirell, but he looked up at the cross and said "Peace". Even now as I write these words, it is hard for me not to shed a tear thinking of just how unselfishly Arthur lived. He then added, "Pope Francis loves peace...so do I." "Well Arthur", I said, "I am ordering a brick with just one word on it – Peace. Then when I sit in the prayer garden and see it, I will think of you, Pope Francis and Jesus' love."

Lord, make me an instrument of your peace.

Where there is hatred let me sow love.

Where there is injury, pardon.

Where there is doubt, faith.

Where there is despair, hope.

Where there is darkness, light

and where there is sadness, joy.

O Divine Master, grant that I may always seek

Not so much to be consoled as to console

To be understood as to understand

To be loved as to love with all my soul.

For it is in giving that we receive

It is in pardoning that we are pardoned

And it is in dying that we're born to eternal life.

(Prayer of St. Francis)

Splashes of Love

Where is God? Everywhere!! That wonderful simple word answer tells us that God's love – "Grace" – is everywhere. It is "splashed" throughout the universe in:

a sunset

a rainy day

a smile

an act of charity

and as Brian Doyle in The Best Spiritual Writing in 2001 said:

"Grace...maybe it lives in us and is activated by illness of Spirit."

How do we dare believe that an illness can energize or give birth to Grace? I truly believe Arthur was God's instrument of Grace here on earth. He told me once, "I wait for God's love every day". He said it didn't always arrive early in the morning when he struggled to get up. In other words, even at times when Arthur felt empty, depleted, or weary, he just believed that God's love would come. I asked, "How would you know when God's love has arrived?" He replied,

"You believe you can get up
when you are weary,
you put your shoes on and
let the laces hang out untied,
you miss a meal and
eat the old crackers you have,
you get to the program where
they serve you a good meal,
and then you smile and thank God
for the wonderful grace-filled day."

Arthur did not just focus on getting to the program and the good meal...all the steps to get there were God's grace – in the strength to get up, get his shoes on and even eating old crackers. Interestingly, these steps were the radiant grace born out of an illness of spirit (schizophrenia), that deprived him at times of any sense of peace and socialization. He never denied that he had struggles; he courageously and heroically embraced them as part of the holy garment of his life.

I now understand what Arthur meant when he shared about "waiting for God's love". It would be in the daily exercise of getting up, getting out, and believing that all of life is fueled with grace...and when we don't deny any hardships, setbacks, or loss as part of life we will find God's love everywhere. You might call that a radical reverence of life.

So often we question a hardship, a detour, a loss and cry out, "why God?!" Perhaps Arthur is showing us the "road less traveled" – the road of believing when it is so difficult – the road of deep faithfulness of spirit that despite any fear, sorrow, or severe disability – it is never too empty to be filled with the grace of acceptance, hope, joy, and simplicity of spirit.

One day, Arthur told me he got home from a walk in the rain and had to take his shoes off and change his socks. His shoes had holes in them. I told him it must have felt good to put on dry socks. Guess what he said? "I walked in a big puddle and the water ripples showed different colors like a rainbow...it made me so happy to see that. I didn't care that my feet got wet". Arthur might have wet feet...but he has the wonderful memory of the splashes of God's grace.

Divine Grace will always speak to an open heart...an open, <u>humble</u> heart. What an example Arthur can be to all of us that in any person and in all types of weather and experiences with our human condition, let us not fear our flaws or limitations, but rather see them as a means of grace for us to refine our way of "living" and "becoming" a spirit or splash of Jesus' love here on earth.

(Romans 8:35-38)

What will separate us from the love of Christ?...For I am convinced neither death, nor life, nor angels, nor principalities, nor present things, nor future things, nor powers, nor height, nor any other creature will be able to separate us from the love of God in Christ Jesus our Lord."

A Hurricane

A few years ago, Hurricane Sandy (2012) hit the Eastern coast causing all kinds of destruction. People found themselves overnight turned upside down ~~ losses, more losses and tragic circumstances to deal with no matter how "unwanted".

My friend Arthur lived in a group home in the Rockaways and was no stranger to the hurricane devastation. He and his group home residents had to be evacuated to safer areas. Arthur found himself on lists to go to various shelters until he was able to return to his main residence. It was indeed a very trying time being moved from place to place. Arthur would call me and never complain. He would tell me this must be where God wants me to be now. He did tell me he found it difficult to go to sleep and he missed his own room.

I kept giving him emotional support as the phone calls increased ~~ I realized that our "connection" was a lifeline for Arthur. I would tell him what I was doing every day. He would say he really appreciated being able to call. The day he arrived back at his own residence he called to tell me Jesus got him home, along with my prayers and support. I smiled and was ever so happy to be a cheerleader for Arthur. But, I thought, it's Arthur's "faithfulness" that really got him back home.

The most vulnerable in our society are people like Arthur who rely on social programs and peoples' good will to enable those with mental illness to get up every day, take their medication, see doctors and go to programs for human development. I believe people with special needs teach us by their courage in daily adversities, to get up every day, to engage when you're tired, to get up when you feel defeated and believe trying again and again is the way to live life ~~giving up is not an option.

No hurricane in life would ever devastate Arthur's goodness. His life was grace under pressure. His gentle countenance that hid mental turmoil at times was the calming of the storm. Arthur survived a hurricane and more in his life~~he believed in a good tomorrow because of how he lived so valiantly today~~all with knowing Jesus love was right there by his side.

Arthur's Favorite Parable

With A Winged Heart

(A Parable about the Bird With Two Broken Wings)

It was a truly wonderful life

soaring above the trees

between the mountains

and gently skimming

the lakes and streams.

It was an adventuresome life

flying from city to city

state to state

and even to foreign countries.

Landing on trees

nesting in backyards

sitting on rooftops

and even in church bell towers.

Flying with friends, strangers

and companions…the bird loved

the freedom, the vistas

that lay ahead with its

changing seasons

of migration and return.

Circling the globe…the bird

learned much about life

in small towns, bustling cities

and even in war-torn countries.

The bird discovered that flying was

such a freeing and carefree experience.

Perhaps it was the very

energy of soaring to new heights

discovering new trails

that enabled the bird to feel ever so happy,

peace-filled and contented.

All is so often…taken in stride

taken for granted

and just merely accepted

as a constant way of life.

But ahhh…

The bird was to encounter a change
a brutal change…a detour
in the bird's mission…to be
a missionary…an explorer…a pioneer.

Perhaps looking back
the bird might truly hum…
was this the whisper
of the mighty wind?
Was the grounding experience
to be a saving grace?

Perhaps…

But what lay ahead of the bird
was the journey.
The journey of acceptance…

acceptance of pain, change

and a total dislocation

of one's being.

One's dreams, hopes, desires

and most of all

one's security…the space of freedom

dignity, and creativity lost…

and perhaps to be reclaimed

in new ways.

How…hummed the bird,

did this happen to me

and why now?

In the prime of my life…

flying so high in the heavens

and touching so gently the stars.

Beholding the Universe

on one's own wings

was truly an awesome,

holy and happy experience

to end so abruptly

and painfully

beleaguered the bird's drooping spirits.

For he had broken both

of his wings

daring to fly

in a turbulent storm

risking too much

feeling so secure

in the insecurities of life's

devastating and harrowing

experiences.

The bird soared

into a mountain peak

hidden by a fog

plunging the bird

at a devastating speed

to earth

barely surviving…
gasping and grappling
for the energy
to lift one's wings
even just one wing
back into flight.

But alas…the wings were cruelly
broken and torn apart
and felt lifeless.

The bird struggled
to crawl
to a small nook of
comfort and safety
to ride the storm out.

Sunlight…Hope
and a chance to mend
one's wings brought
a very painful discovery

that the bird

would forever remain

wounded…broken…impaired.

What the bird thought…

no more flights

soaring into the

blue skies…and traveling.

What would…could

a bird do

who was grounded?

Birds were made for

flying high above the earth.

Fear…a terrible fear

filled the bird's heart and

his drooping spirit ached

more and more each day.

Try as he could…the wings

felt heavy, lifeless

and sad.

The experience plunged the bird

into a dark space in life…

he hid…isolated and

berated this terrible ordeal.

As time went on

the bird thought…

what am I to do all day long…

and all night long…

die of suffering

or look around this grounded space

and discover

some kind of new mission?

But inside the bird wondered…

what can a bird do…except fly!

So the bird began what was to be

a very surprising, mysterious

and awesome journey…

The bird knew he would attract the attention

of the townspeople for…

what bird walked around a town all the time!

But thought the bird

it's all I have left or else I will die

or drift into deep loneliness and despair,

something in the bird's heart

gave wings to hope and courage

resiliency and faith.

So, the bird set out visiting the people places

in life…

Awkward at first…the people and the bird marveled

at his appearances at:

laundromats

delicatessens

bakeries

shopping malls

churches, synagogues and mosques

mental health centers and hospitals.

The bird even went to:

libraries

museums

movie theaters

and even to concerts at the park.

After his first daring, and at times,

embarrassing encounters at hearing remarks like:

What's that crazy bird up to?

Why doesn't he use his wings?

Look at the silly bird walking around a laundromat!

The bird felt the disdain, mocking and humiliation

of being a wingless bird in flight.

But soon the townspeople were to discover

that the wounded bird only wanted

to feel wanted, cared for and accepted…

Crumbs of food and bird houses were

set up in the strangest of places

welcoming this wounded flyer…to earth.

The bird always longed for his real home

the clouds, the spires, trees and nests.

But

he realized within his own broken heart and

aching spirit

for what could not be… that he was being given

another chance at life,

to find life anew in the misfortunes…in the pain

and also in the courage to survive change, loss

and hardship.

Not easy…for a bird that longed for his

companion birds…

many a tear he wept in solitude.

It was a strange way to embrace

his broken wings

by touching the hearts of the people on earth.

The bird was to learn that very often these

people yearned to fly...

to fly away from life.

At first the bird thought this a

peculiar wish for human beings to want to

fly...surely, that was only for birds!!

But as he listened to their chatter, laughter,

sorrows and sometimes bitterness at the

deli

library

church

school

rehab centers

and on the streets

The bird realized that in some way his broken wings

had been a gift for others.

They saw his disabling condition but they also

saw and felt the bird's determination

to find life in this new disorder.

The bird started to hear people comment

not on his brokenness

but on his ability and tenacity

to steer a new course.

"If that bird can do it, so can I!"

"That bird has guts (he learned that meant courage)."

This made the bird feel affirmed

understood and even respected.

It was the night he spent on the park bench

with the two homeless men…whom he discovered

had not just an extra bottle to share…

but had **compassion** in each other's misfortunes

and even with the bird.

The bird encountered these two homeless men
one lonely evening on his nightly stroll when
all or most of the townspeople were tucked away
in their warm homes (that the bird called nests).

The bird sat next to the two men and listened to their
reminiscing about the past
and what could have been…
they included the bird as they too had heard
of the bird with the two broken wings…

"Well, little bird", one of the men said…
"you might not be able to fly
but you certainly have gained
the esteem of this town…
you dare to walk among us different,
wounded and courageous
despite your fears".

"Why, we even have heard how
you attend church services

in various holy places…

and hum sweet melodies of peace, hope and

compassion…

now that is a mighty fine mission".

The bird listened with his heart

and even shed a tear or two.

This made the man touch the bird

with a gentle caress and say:

"You, little bird along with my homeless companion,

are the only ones who have cared enough to cry

with me and for me…

I feel warmed by your tenderness and mercy.

Somehow, I feel encouraged…why,

I do believe, I'll give flight to my life again."

The two men patted the bird a good night gesture

and what would really become of these

two homeless men the bird was not really sure.

What the bird did know was that being grounded

and deprived of what was so much a part

of his life…flying

had brought him to a "sacred space"

of letting go…

and letting God lead the bird with the

two broken wings to an unassuming

and very surprising new ground.

Where the bird would meet the ordinary,

extraordinary, the holy and

the secular and be able to

"look up" and give

flight

to his heart that so much yearned for

new life.

This new ground was his home…

his nesting place…

Where he would walk among the people

and their broken spirits

and find great gifts

of tenderness, joy and deep peace.

Who ever thought a bird…
who had once soared so sigh…and free
could find contentment
being grounded and surrounded
by humanity.

The daily walks revealed
to the bird all the broken dreams,
lost identities and the struggles
for peace of these worldly creatures.

The bird had found a precious gift
that was no longer his to own…
but rather to give away.

It was the gift of **acceptance**
whatever space, condition or circumstances
we find ourselves in.
We can learn that in Faith and with Faith

that we will in our brokenness continue on our life's

journey.

Believing…believing greatly in a power

beyond ourselves

that any tears, disappointments,

setbacks and even tragedies

can be turned into joy…

a joy that gives meaning to life.

At the close of this parable…

The bird sets off in a new direction

to visit a refugee center where

people have suffered and

seek healing.

This is where I shall walk today

thought the bird…and perhaps

I shall give wings to another

broken heart

for this is my mission and it is

grounded…in love

in God's love…eternal love.

And with this thought in mind…the bird looked up

to the heavens to see his flock in flight…and

he did not cry…

he smiled…with deep thanks for

knowing that all of life is a gift.

(I hope as you journeyed with the bird with

two broken wings…you were able to identify with

some loss…great or small in life…

and give wings of hope and joy

to your journey and where it has led you thus far.)

(Sister Ave Clark, O.P.)

The Bird with the Two Broken Wings
Parable

"Trust in the Lord at all times and
pour out your hearts before our God
...who is our refuge" (Psalm 62:6-9)

Heart-Reflection Questions

How do you embrace the changes that life offers you?

How do you dare to journey through pain, loss and fear to discover meaning?

Have you ever shared deep caring for another person's struggles and found yourself transformed?

When you arrive at the sacred space of acceptance of your life's journey...what gifts of light can you acknowledge?

Are you willing to listen with hearts of compassion to the call to "let go"...and trod a new path called challenge, inspiration and transformation?

Write your own Heart-Reflection

Arthur's Prayer:

<u>Lord of Faith</u>: walk gently with me and surround me with your light…to step into life knowing that Jesus' presence will give wings to my love…this is my hope and my prayer…to remain steadfast in seeking my Lord in my ordinary life. Amen.

Change the World

One evening while on the phone with Arthur, I asked him, "How do you change the world for the better"? "Let me see", he said. "I don't take for granted those who care for me. I appreciate getting a freshly baked bagel at Dunkin Donuts. I thank God for the sky so I can look up and greet a new day." "Oh Arthur", I said, "you are teaching me how to change the world for the better by your daily and ordinary deeds, attitudes, caring ways, words of appreciation, love, respect and reverence for all of life".

Arthur liked to get up early and go out for a walk. He would stop along the way and thank the sanitation men who pick up paper, garbage and recycling products. He would greet the mailman and crossing guard with a wave of good morning.

By Arthur's daily attitude of welcome, he made the world a better place to live in by looking up and seeing the mantle of God's love so blue in the day

---

and so starry at night. In his every day and ordinary actions, Arthur changed my world. Thank you for being Jesus' all-inclusive love. Gift of Grace...Gift of God~~that's who we can be for one another.

Everyone is our neighbor~~next-door, across the street, around the corner. North~East~South~West, across the ocean via plane, ship, car, train, scooter, skates, skateboard and hiking boots. Humanity is our neighbor~~diverse in many ways, so very human-gifted, talented, flawed, limited, joyful, sorrowful, happy, sad, challenged and inspired.

What would the world look like, feel like and become **if** each one of us took Arthur's example and dared to change the world by making it a better, kinder, compassionate, all-embracing place to live. The world could become a place of patience and hope, charity and respect, peace, empathy and faithfulness. Let's change the world!!

Is it possible? Arthur told me YES! I believe his early morning legacy of greeting others with one kind word, one welcoming look, one respectful nod, one tear of hope and one gentle embrace of compassion tells us how to change the world for the better. I believe, like Arthur, we all get a chance, and an opportunity every day to be and become a seed that sows wonderful peace-filled love.

A Parish with a Beautiful Heart

The Diocese of Brooklyn, New York has many beautiful churches; some are more than 100 years old. The tall steeples stand over crowded streets with exquisitely carved stone crosses, statues, and communion rails. History lives in the art work and sacred sanctuaries of these parishes.

One parish that I go to was founded in 1961...a simple structure of more modern-day architecture. What makes St. Jude's a parish with a heart is not the exterior landscaped shrubbery or the carved stone or the interior religious art work. St. Jude's has a sacred ingredient ~~ a beautiful welcome reflected in the faces, spirit, and hearts of its multi-cultural community. This was the parish Arthur arrived in over a decade ago to worship, become a Catholic convert and a very active member of the church's spiritual organizations.

The people of St. Jude's have deep faith. For years I have been going there to offer evenings of prayer. By the time I would arrive, the parishioners had the room ready with chairs arranged and a side table setup with cake and coffee for all to enjoy. When Arthur attended, the people would make sure he had a chair and a cup of coffee.

The people of St. Jude's welcomed Arthur and helped him to become a member of their various societies ~~ Holy Name Society, Nocturnal Adoration Society and Apostolate of Prayer, to name a few. Arthur never missed a meeting or a chance to sign up for 24-hour Adoration. In fact, Arthur stayed all night so no hour was left unattended. The parishioners were very respectful to him and his special needs. They accompanied him to meetings as friends. Arthur called them his "Jesus friends and his Catholic family". Everyone knew him. He was the gentle man they saw praying in church at all hours .

Arthur would smile when he told me how much he enjoyed the parish parties and celebrations. He also showed me all the holy cards he had collected over the years -- each one had a special meaning for him. Very often, the cards came from some religious event at the church.

I wrote this chapter about St. Jude's because I know how much Arthur appreciated this community. He often spoke about Father Mike Tedone and Msgr. John Delendick. Arthur said they served Mass so reverently and their homilies were like Jesus speaking. Arthur also expressed how fond he was of his dear friend, Sister Mary Stiefvater the pastoral assistant. Arthur knew Sister Mary had great compassion and understanding of his illness. He often told me Sister Mary is like Mother Mary – I agreed.

His special friends, Nina and Pete, (Pete is in heaven now), Celeste and Joanne were graces of love in his life. He especially was grateful to Celeste for being his teacher and companion in the RCIA program. When Arthur became a Catholic, Celeste was his sponsor. They walked down the aisle together at the Easter Vigil. Arthur told me later that he felt she was his guardian angel.

You can see and feel from this chapter that St. Jude's parish has a beautiful heart because of the ministers and the people. When you enter the church, there are handmade posters created by Nina announcing different parish events. The simplicity, genuine caring and sharing of presence are what decorates this parish. How blessed Arthur was to find such a parish and what a blessing Arthur was for them.

Friendship

We all have a friend(s) with whom we feel we can "just be" who we are~~with our flaws, gifts and those daily human inconsistencies. A friend is someone we can care deeply about, look to for advice and guidance or call just to say hello. Friends make us smile, cry, laugh or shed a tear. They share all the emotions of daily living: losses embraced and successes celebrated. A friend makes you feel comfortable with and truly grateful for life...a friend is someone you treasure and hope to remember--forever in your heart.

Arthur and I became <u>good</u> <u>friends.</u> Our phone conversations over the years were like the unwrapping of wonderful sunsets and sunrises. They were a pool of feelings shared with hope, faith, suffering, struggles, happiness and trust to name a few.

Arthur had a wonderful gift of speaking his truth in ways that were never demanding, angry or despairing. He would share with me his zig-zag journey of his life with schizophrenia. Arthur would not cover up the struggles this mental illness would visit upon him from time to time. A few times when he was hospitalized, Arthur would call me telling me he would get "healing" help at the hospital. I would focus in on the word "healing" and ask him what kind of "healing" would the hospital stay give him. Oh, "<u>wonderful healing</u>" he would say along with medication, diet, exercise, and good chats on the phone. He would also add that "great kindness" was the best healer~~to go the extra mile, the extra step, to go out of your way to ensure someone's safety; to befriend every aspect of a friend's life, even those events/experiences that are so painful and never ending. Arthur <u>understood</u> the beautiful meaning of friendship~~a sacred treasure to cherish forever.

I Knew You Before I Met You

When I first met Arthur, it was at an evening of prayer at a parish in Brooklyn. I gave my card to him and he asked if he could call me. I said, "Yes". Then he asked me what time I would get home. I smiled and told him about 9:45 P.M. He called at 10:00 P.M. and that would be the wonderful beginning of phone calls every day for 12 years. It was also the wonderful beginning of a heart to heart friendship.

On that first evening phone call, he told me he enjoyed the evening of prayer and liked the songs and prayers I shared. Then he said "I knew you before I met you." I wasn't sure what he meant so I asked, "How do you know me?" He told me that he read a book that I had written for healing from abuse and violence entitled, Lights in the Darkness. I took his knowing me as a compliment, but also as a soul-spirit. I said, "I am glad that you liked the book". He said, "it helped me ~~ your courage saved me."

I was quiet. I smiled as a tear rolled down my face. "Arthur, you are a valiant man...a survivor. Good for you and keep on". He told me he would always keep on as that was the best path to take ~~to go forward. I agreed. I have often thought of Arthur telling me he knew me before he met me. Sometimes we read a book, an article, see a video someone made and enjoy it; feel a sense of unity with the author and appreciate how they communicate their message. That feels so healing.

One evening I asked Arthur, "Do you know Jesus?" He replied, "Yes, I knew him from an early age. I was walking past a church in Brooklyn where there was a carnival. The pastor waved to me and pointed at the hot dogs and the rides ~~ he welcomed me. I knew he was Jesus' love for me. "Here is the wonderful example: Arthur saw Jesus' love in people who showed kindness in words, deeds and actions. This is who we are. We are all called to be and become the image of Jesus' love made evident in this world. "And the word became flesh" (John 1:14).

I asked Arthur how homeless people are Jesus' love in the world. He told me homeless people:

~ hold a cup in their hand with humility for a heart offering

~ sometimes they hold signs that say "Thank You-God Bless You"

~ know how to help people and tell them where to get a free cup of coffee or soup

~ teach us to trust

~ have strength despite set backs

~ help us to be compassionate as Jesus was

~ have Faith

Yes Arthur, I agree.

He then went on to say that at times he felt homeless, I sensed a deep sadness when he shared this. I asked him what do you do with that sadness...he smiled (Arthur had a good sense of humor) and said "sometimes I go to Dunkin Donuts!" We both laughed. "Well", I said, "a nice toasted bagel with cream cheese can sure ease some sadness." After our laugh, he told me he never wanted his sadness to make him bitter. He said the best place to take his sadness was to go to the church's Prayer Garden (which is the place Arthur and I visited the day before he passed away).

At the garden, which he called the Peace Garden, Arthur would sit quietly and not think about how sad, hurt or fearful he was. He would sit and thank Jesus for sitting with him. To me that is a blessing. Arthur's example of believing that Jesus is there in every feeling of sadness, hurt and loss was a saving grace. Just sitting quietly, reflecting and meditating at the Peace Garden brought Arthur wonderful solace. Peace, not that this world can give, but that Jesus' love can give.

As Arthur sat and prayed, he told me he felt Jesus was showing him how to live in a new way (a new perspective) and God was using his pain and struggle to be a sign of joy and hope for the world. He told me about his "new way" so humbly and sincerely. I now try to integrate Arthur's "new way" into my life journey and like Arthur I marvel at the mystery of Jesus' love that is revealed to humanity when we are willing to listen and learn from the most vulnerable among us. Perhaps this "new way" embraced in ordinary deeds will help you and I get to know Jesus through Arthur's holy life.

<u>Lights In The Darkness</u>
by Sister Ave Clark, O.P.
Catholic Book Publishing Company

The Listening Heart

How do you listen? When do you listen? Why do you listen? To whom do you listen? Do you really listen?

When we listen to another person's opinion, thoughts, hopes, and dreams, what do we hear? How do we listen when someone has a strong or different opinion or way of looking at a worldview than we do?

I am just as human as others ~~ we all want people to agree with what we are saying or feeling. How do we listen with our heart? I must tell you I learned a lot about listening when Arthur and I would have our six or seven chats a day over 12 years. I learned to listen to every word, the feelings shared amidst fragmented thoughts.

I learned to listen with quiet respect. I learned to listen without always understanding everything shared...I listened with compassion.

I learned to listen to what was important to Arthur. I listened with enthusiasm. I learned to listen to feelings of abandonment, deep hurt and frustrations of living with schizophrenia. I learned to listen with a comforting heart.

Arthur was a great listener. If someone was sad or tearful, Arthur would tell me he listened to their tears and sorrows. Arthur also had a wonderful sense of humor and laughter that sounded like "pure joy". He would listen to a story that made him laugh and then tell me he felt so happy his heart was dancing with joy. Every aspect of 'Arthur's listening heart was a gift~~even the sincere unraveling of feelings. I would ask a question to get him back on track and Arthur would say, "thank you for getting me back on track so respectfully. I appreciate your listening even when I get mixed up." "Arthur", I said, "I will always listen to you." He replied, "Sr. Ave, I have a smile on my face because of what you just said." Because of Arthur, I now listen to smiles:

Smiles of a baby

Smiles of a small child

Smiles of a busy teenager

Smiles of an adult

Smiles of an elder

To listen is to go to the center of our being and listen with a heart spirit that accepts, embraces, beholds, touches, gazes, does not judge and gives a respectful hug.

Listening is like weaving a garment of Jesus' love...its' colors vary and the texture of the garment changes through all the seasons of life. It is always there waiting to be worn, shared and celebrated. Listening is like being the heartbeat of Jesus' love.

In listening, we bring optimism to our world, hope to our relationships and diversity of joy to our celebrations. Like Jesus, Arthur had these wonderful gifts. Arthur's listening had an extraordinary quality called Peace. No wound or sorrow would bind him to any worldly rejection. Rather, Arthur was freed to really listen with peace, charity, patience and a love that endures forever and ever.

Thank you, Arthur, for giving everyone with whom you met...a piece of your "listening heart".

The Cross

<u>Lift High the Cross</u>. How does one do this when its' burden weighs you down? How do you embrace the cross? Some crosses are announced and we are prepared (as much as we can be). Some crosses come unannounced and suddenly we find ourselves in turmoil, deep sorrow, illness, painful accident injuries, heart-breaking loss that tosses us into a struggle to find the strength, even the hope to lift up our cross...to lift up our very life. Arthur embraced his cross as a disciple of holy courage.

I remember asking Arthur if it was all right to ask him questions about his life journey. He would tell me that he liked when I asked about his life; it means I was interested in his well-being. "That I am, Arthur", I said smiling.

He told me that he was diagnosed with schizophrenia in his late teens. He said at first, he thought the disease would go away; but instead it escalated and life changed quite drastically for him. Despite being very smart and enjoying reading great books, the emotional roller coaster of schizophrenia took a toll in Arthur's life...no more schooling and his social life collapsed.

The Cross. Ups and downs, changes and more loss. Arthur survived. The call of the sacred was a healing space for Arthur. He told me looking at the cross or doing the Stations of the Cross reminded him of how much Jesus loves each one of us. Arthur knew Jesus loved him no matter what his human condition.

Arthur's faith was his holy anchor. If he was too tired or emotionally weary and wasn't up to saying the rosary...he would just hold the cross.

In very human and heroic ways, Arthur befriended and lifted up his cross. He became an inspiration to others. His heart-peace bore his cross as Christ's love did on Calvary ~~ an amazing grace. Let us together lift up our crosses.

Living a Prayer

"Whoever is in Christ is a new creation"

(2Cor 5:17)

It was Lent and Arthur called me that he was on a bus taking him to a Lenten evening of prayer in a parish in Rockaway, NY. When he arrived, he would call me again and tell me that he was in church and the choir was practicing. I could hear the beautiful voices singing praises to God. Arthur told me he loved to go early to the church and listen to the choir singing. It made him feel safe, comforted and in God's presence.

In his attendance at Mass, retreats and stations of the cross, Arthur found great solace; he became one with his prayers and these feelings spilled over into Arthur's daily living experience. Arthur became Jesus' love:

~   by accepting others just as they are

~   patience with life's stumbling blocks

- ~ compassion for others' sufferings
- ~ joyful for, with, and to others
- ~ accepting of life's adversities
- ~ valiant in carrying his cross
- ~ respectful of others' limitations especially those with mental illness
- ~ appreciation for any small kindness
- ~ having a welcoming heart
- ~ being a faithful friend

The above could be the "Ten Commandments of Arthur's Goodness".

I gave Arthur rosary beads blessed by Pope Francis. Arthur told me he held the holy beads each evening when sleep would not come to him. When he feels the weariness of his illness, he would hold the beads next to his heart. Arthur would just hold his prayers and his faith...he would rely on Jesus' love to comfort him in any tribulation.

Because of his struggles, Arthur understood the human condition of weakness, loss, pain, sorrow, tragedy and limitations. He also understood quite deeply how rejection, abandonment, cruelty and harsh words could cause deep hurts and deep wounds. Because of his inner spirit of loving Jesus, Arthur did not just memorize or recite prayers and attend religious services. He took his prayer life out into the public, into the streets, on buses, in stores (especially Dunkin Donuts) and at his residence.

Arthur was a living prayer. He will continue to be a light ~~ a quiet, unassuming, hidden, humble and holy light! What a wonderful way to live your life.

Arthur bore his cross with a courageous integrity of spirit. I told him quite a few times that he was an example of being a faithful follower of Jesus ~~ always sincere in sharing kindness from an open heart, a humble heart that reflected in living his prayer life~~

the very face of Jesus love full of mercy and compassion.

(When Arthur passed away, his Pope Francis rosary beads were right next to him.)

The Blessing of Vulnerability

We live in a society that sometimes discriminates concerning people with vulnerable needs. We only focus on their needs and how that affects society. Arthur's life and demeanor reflected deep vulnerability mirroring all his social, physical and emotional needs. Arthur was far more than any human need.

If only people would truly take time to know individuals like Arthur, then they would discover themselves in a new dimension. If only we would not fear our own vulnerability (we all have it!!)~~stop hiding it, ignoring it, or fleeing from it. If only we would take time to be truly a human being with vulnerabilities and find in this wonderful discovery a resilience of the human spirit. Arthur did just that ... he was a gentleman with trials that never diminished his inner goodness.

When I would tell Arthur he was very courageous and good-hearted despite the effects schizophrenia had on is life, he told me he had some great examples of how to embrace suffering:

~ people in AA--what courage to face addiction and become a healing source for others

~ survivors of abuse and violence – daring to speak the truth and give us examples of being valiant

~ soldiers returning from combat – wounded by terrors and stepping into the light of courageous healing

~ a courageous and faithful soul – is reborn after loss, illness, tragedy; scarred but blessed by hope

~ people with mental illness (like Arthur) living each day, accepting help and connecting to life

If only we could all see ourselves or someone we love on this list of people who show us how to live courageously, faithfully and with love for one another. Thank you, Arthur, for being Jesus' loving example.

One evening during one of our phone conversations Arthur and I were discussing where we see and feel hope when feeling vulnerable. I sincerely believe Arthur's list will bring a smile to your hope and healing to your vulnerability. Here is Arthur's definition of hope:

~ a smile from a stranger in a store

~ a welcome chair and table at a church party

~ a friend saying "I care"

~ accepting a candle to light a feeling of poverty

~ a listening heart on the phone'

~ a handshake of peace

~ a ride home in the evening

~ being invited to a friend's home

I can only imagine the divine smile of Jesus as Arthur shared his belief that hope is born in every ordinary act of kindness.

No reason to ignore our vulnerabilities...perhaps to see them as blessings is to see with the gaze of Jesus' love:

- ~ to not fear another person's differences
- ~ to know our smiles can shed a tear
- ~ to be able to sit peacefully and comfortably with another person in a Peace Garden
- ~ to be a very human person and learn from your own or someone else that a vulnerability usually has a gift

Imagine if like Arthur we could say...

"Thank you, Jesus, I am human, very human. I am vulnerable, very vulnerable. I am holy and today I am be-coming a blessing of hope for myself and for every person I will meet."

Arthur, you will be a forever blessing
in my life.

My Favorite Mystery

"We also glory in our suffering because we know that suffering produces perseverance (James 5:3)

I was given a pair of rosary beads blessed by Pope Francis in a case with the pope's image on it. I told Arthur that I would like to give them to him. "Oh Sister", he said, "I would be honored to have those beads." I asked Arthur what was his favorite Mystery of the rosary to say and he said the Sorrowful Mysteries. I was hoping he would say the Joyful Mysteries. I guess that would have made me happy. I asked him why he chose the Sorrowful. He told me the Sorrowful Mysteries tell you just how much Jesus loves us. "You are so right", I said. He went on to say the fourth Sorrowful Mystery touched him so deeply ~~ the carrying of the cross. Arthur knew Jesus was helping him to carry his cross every day. Praying about Jesus carrying the cross helped Arthur feel that he too could carry his cross even when it felt too heavy to bear. He added, "You Sister are my Simon of Cyrene as I struggle to carry my cross".

I was deeply touched and asked Arthur, "how am I your Simon of Cyrene". He answered "your compassionate heart-listening helps me". As always, I was humbled by Arthur's sincere words. Arthur gives us a holy reminder that the Jesus in you and me (and Arthur) is the love that lifts us up, encourages us and empowers each one of us not to be overcome by any trial or weariness of spirit. What is your favorite Mystery of the Rosary and why? Is there something in that Mystery that helps you feel, live and love Jesus more?

Why not go to the Sorrowful Mysteries and dare to befriend your own sorrow and disappointment, failure or fear and find the amazing grace of a loving Jesus carrying the cross to Calvary. This is where we can find Jesus in all unexpected and perhaps unwanted detours in life.

Let us like Arthur dare to touch the mystery of God's unconditional love and carry our cross everyday trusting and believing in a wonderful resurrection. Let us as we carry Jesus' love believe in the ordinary and the extraordinary graces offered to us.

A friend told me after she read the article in the 'Tablet' about Arthur's passing that she wouldn't think of Arthur resting in peace but rather risen in glory. She sincerely believed (so do I) that Arthur showed all of us that sorrow touched by Jesus love is a beautiful mystery. Because of Arthur we can all understand a bit more about the glory of the cross.

Blazing Charity

I gave Arthur a book about a "little" Dominican named Blessed Margaret of Castello. I told him that like Jesus, Margaret lived only 33 years here on earth. He asked me why I sent him the book. "Oh Arthur", I said, "pray to Blessed Margaret. She, like you, lived so courageously with her disabilities."

I told him that she was born quite disfigured – blind, lame and hunchback. She grew up feeling rejection and abandonment, but always remained faithful. After Arthur read the book, he told me that Margaret of Castello's life, despite being subjected to some hurts, was truly a life of "blazing charity". I had never heard of charity being described as "blazing". He then told me that as he read about her life story, he was so taken by her inner charity even for those who were not so kind to her. He felt it was as if she was consumed by the fire of love – a blazing love.

Whenever I was with Arthur or chatting on the phone with him, I felt that I was being embraced by his blazing charity. His kind words sometimes told me of how he spent his day by encouraging other residents, sharing a Dunkin Donut gift card or giving his warm gloves to someone sitting outside. Arthur freely chose to be a kind loving person not just on easy days or in comfortable ways. Arthur freely chose to be a beautiful heart always. He looked at life with an open trusting heart no matter what was happening in his life.

Light comes in through the cracks of any darkness. I know Arthur always found that light no matter how slight or dim it was. He saw the small moment, the unasked-for kindness as Jesus' blazing charity living within him. Like Blessed Margaret, I believe Arthur was and will continue to be a blessing to all who got to know him through his words, deeds, and actions. Just think, if everyone set out each day showering the world with an extra act of goodness, a word of affirmation, or prayer turned outward for peace and reconciliation in our community, our whole world would then be untied in "blazing charity."

Arthur did not just turn to God when faced with a difficulty or a worldly mystery; he was united with God's love 24/7. How do I know this? I was the recipient of being a friend – a heart friend with Arthur. Our years of phone chats became for <u>both</u> of us prayer chats of trust, laughter, kindness, compassion, and comfort. Messages left on my answering machine brought a smile to my spirit. Arthur can now be our holy ambassador of peace, hope, and joy. As we reflect on his way of life, we begin to realize that anyone who genuinely loves God will travel securely.

Arthur can show us how to think, see, and feel the loving kindness of God in our life. Don't hold on to it so tightly; be like Arthur and give it away for in doing so we all become a wonderful spark of the "blazing charity" of Jesus' love.

"We are blessed, not according to our work, but according to the measure of our love."
(St. Catherine of Sienna)

The Life of Blessed Margaret of Castello
By Father W. Bonniwell, O.P.
(Tan Books, Charlotte, North Carolina)

The Gift of Holy Appreciation

Arthur told me he was going to turn 70 years old in 2016 and this would be the beginning of a new decade of adventure. To Arthur, age was a holy journey. What he felt was more days to thank Jesus. I decided to plan a party for Arthur. I invited some people from St. Jude's parish where Arthur was a member before he had to move. Everyone offered to bring something – plates, napkins, soda, chips – and I made a yellow birthday cake, the flavor Arthur chose.

On the day of the party, each person brought a gift and card for Arthur. Before they presented these to him, they said something in prayer, poetry or words from their heart.

"Thank you for your brave heart"

"Thank you for your prayerful life

that inspires all of us"

"Thank you for always being so thoughtful"

"Thank you for teaching us how to be so accepting of life's crosses"

As Arthur received the gifts and opened the cards, he looked at each person and told them how deeply grateful he was for the present and what they said about him. Then he told each of them that he loved them in Jesus' name for making his 70th birthday so very special and joyful.

As he spoke with such simplicity and sincerity, tears filled the eyes of all the listeners. You could feel the presence of holy
appreciation in Arthur's words. As everyone was leaving and thanking me for hosting such a wonder-ful birthday party, I smiled and said, "Arthur hosted the party with his tender appreciation." They all agreed with a smile as they touched their hearts.

So, what really is appreciation? After Arthur's party, I knew appreciation is not just the fast unwrapping of gifts and saying thank you. No, <u>holy appreciation</u> looks into the heart of the giver and bestows loving thanks. It takes time, embraces the moment deeply, affirms the giver simply and blesses the acceptance of what is given. This type of appreciation is centered in a soul that sees the sacred in giving and receiving. It comes from an open heart, from a receiver who is ever joyful, full of gratitude for presence being shared and a heart that leaves a "spiritual hug-print" of love in our very soul.

All who attended Arthur's 70th birthday party were truly the receivers of this wonderful gift of holy appreciation. Through Arthur's example, all of us can share holy appreciation when we are given opportunities to receive joy, peace, love, comfort, hope, healing and great caring. Perhaps we can all whisper when these ordinary opportunities come into our life "Thank you, Arthur, for being Jesus' love."

A Beautiful Soul

There are people in life you meet that touch the depths of your very being...they leave a wonderful heart-print of compassion on your very soul. You are forever changed because of their inner goodness. They are not rich, self-important or famous for any inventions or collected material wealth.

These "good" people are selfless in giving, sharing, caring, hoping...these people live the very essence and meaning of Jesus' call to:

"Love one another as He has loved us"

What do these people do that sets them apart...they shine their goodness... it is not so much in what they do but rather in <u>who they are</u>...who they have become...no beauty shines brighter than that of a compassionate heart.

One of these shining lights in my life was Arthur. Despite any of his struggles, Arthur never poured out his sorrows, losses or hurts on anyone. In fact, whenever he shared any of his difficulties with me…it was never in a complaining mode. No, he usually was asking me to pray for him or telling me how he was going to get up and go out ~~ change his space…isn't that a creative way of dealing with a problem? Don't just sit and mope with it…go take a walk~~and life will unfold in new ways. Arthur would tell me he was <u>walking with Jesus</u>.

Indeed, my dear friend very often would take a walk to his church four blocks away and sit on a bench in the church's Prayer Garden. He would just be quiet and listen to nature…and listen to God~~in the silence Arthur heard the message of love…

"I will always be with you…do not fear"
Arthur had a beautiful spiritual connection to the Father, Son and Holy Spirit. Faith made a great and

holy difference in Arthur's life. His open heart was a gift for himself and all those who knew him...by his openness to Jesus' call, "Come Follow Me". Arthur was transformed ~~ he became a beautiful soul ~~ a disciple of love. My life is changed because of knowing Arthur ~~

"It is no longer I who live but Christ lives in me".
(Galatians 2:20)

Let each of us open our hearts...let's do it together and transform our world!

A Beautiful Soul

A stained wrinkled plaid shirt
shoelaces untied
buttons buttoned wrong
no socks on in winter
You are a <u>beautiful soul.</u>
You give away a new shirt to someone in need.
You give thanks for your new shoes.
(which you said felt heavenly to walk in)
You smiled at your buttons buttoned wrong.
(you accept your limitations with such grace)
You were in a hurry to get to the retreat
and forgot to put your socks on.
You are a <u>beautiful soul.</u>
The pastor made the coffee for the retreat
Someone said it was way too strong
Arthur smiled and said
"I'll put more milk in the pastor's good coffee".
Like Jesus, Arthur, you lived and shared the way of
goodness.
You are a <u>beautiful soul.</u>

(Sr. Ave Clark, O.P.)

Be the Gentle Face of Jesus' Love

You know what our world needs ~~ more gentleness of sprit. I am sure you have some friends that just by being in their company give you a sense of peace, serenity harmony and calmness of spirit.

My friend Arthur had a gentle spirit, a welcoming heart, and a pleasant personality. Being in Arthur's company was a joy and a caring space to share. It would be in our ordinary conversations that Arthur's wisdom would be shared quietly and very often with inspiring insights.

One day, as I was driving along with Arthur, we stopped to look at what he called 'flowers with beautiful lights' ~~ it was a lawn full of dandelions. Arthur saw in the lawn the face of God's loving light. He told me each little dandelion adds to the beautiful brightness of the lawn. I said, "I guess we are all like these dandelions". "We need each other to share

Jesus' love", he said. Arthur was so right. As we drove away I thought, "like a small dandelion, each one of us can share our light and add to the brightness of life wherever we go".

One evening, Arthur called to say he was going downstairs for a few hours to celebrate the birthdays of the month. He told me he had a card for each person; one of the people had not always been kind to Arthur. He said, "today is his birthday and I want to be the love of Jesus for him". "Ahh", I thought, how many of us would not give a card or even attend a celebration for someone who was rude to us. Arthur saw every day as a **bright new beginning**. To be described as a **gentle soul** is a wonderful compliment. Wouldn't it be great if just one person every day realized that being gentle like Jesus…is actually a sign of living and loving with holy courage?

Gentleness has a way of welcoming, consoling and caring. Gentleness has a quiet unassuming way of being in the world. Gentleness has a sacred space…a deep reverence for all of life. No one is left out of a gentle gaze, a gentle touch, a gentle word…a gentle whisper of Jesus love. Arthur told me he felt his gentleness was God's gift of amazing grace in his life. Arthur saw Jesus' gentleness in the sunrise and sunsets of life…in the getting up and also in the comfort of peace.

One might wonder how this man with the disease of schizophrenia was so gentle. I truly believe his faith and trust were like wings of hope and compassion. To have a spirit so connected to Jesus' love, despite fragmented thoughts and bouts with social and emotional setbacks, tells us in Romans 8 that no matter what happens in life…we are never separated from the love of God…the spark…the very spark of the Divine lives in us and for that we are ever grateful. Arthur's courageous struggles became lights in the darkness for him and for me…his "forever friend".

Whenever I see a dandelion I will be reminded of Arthur's wonderful inner brightness. The brightness we all have to share and become.

The Little Dandelion~~Treasured Forever

(A Parable inspired by Arthur)

There was once a gigantic, large green field nestled in a forest of trees of various sizes and shapes of prominence. The forest was the home for many an animal...small creatures of the Lord; squirrels, raccoons, insects (ugg!) birds, butterflies and even some fish and periodically a roaming cat or dog. It was truly a place of God's creative design where even the leaves, berries, flowers and small emerging buds shared the giftedness of their fragrances that made this forest a special, sacred and beautiful place to live. Many visitors came...children; men and women from everywhere to rest, play and perhaps to just find moments of solitude, peace and hope.

It was here in the forest...that the field of green, so green, was the grass that one would think it was an emerald blanket of creation so deep, so soft and so quietly exquisite. Many a visitor romped on this field of green playing sports, having picnics or just strolling hand in hand. It was on this field that the little dandelion lived…a bright, bright yellow…a symbol of God's sunlight ever present in the midst of such grandeur. For sure as Gerard Manley Hopkins, S.J. (a poet) wrote:

"The world is charged with the grandeur of God."
So too, was this little dandelion.

On stormy days the forest was unusually very, very quiet letting the rain water its very life of streams, roots, soil and hearts. The tall pines would lift up their boughs and receive this water of life in gratitude. The animals would find refuge in a cave, nook or tree watching the rain bringing new life to its' surrounding home.

The little dandelion would feel the waters beating down on its' fragile stalk and lean on the green grass for its protection. After the storm or rain shower the dandelion would appear taller and brighter. It had its special place in this magnificent garden of life. All seemed to live in harmony, respected each other's dignity, uniqueness and connections. It was what one might call...a world of love.

The Little dandelion just always thought and believed this is where I shall dwell forever...but life was to bring changes. Part of the forest had its trees removed and the soil eroded and left a vacancy that no one could fill. The streams were to dry up and some of the fish were removed and saved while others were left to 'eek' out their lives and die.

Some of the animals chatted among themselves of a different life being built in their forest...it was called industry. Was this new technology not taking into consideration that a garden and a forest are places that our world needs to protect, nurture and share with great respect and care. Ahh...no one asked the inhabitants of this tranquil forest what they thought and knew of the beauty and meaning of this holy and sacred place of creation.

And so, bit-by-bit, day-by-day, the noise was not of picnics, children playing games or people strolling; but rather the noise was of bulldozers and concrete buildings and shop after shop called a mall of stores. When all was finished...in place of the trees that had graced the forest with the grandeur of God now stood tall skyscraper buildings called corporations. The emerald green lawn was also being replaced by cement for a multi-tiered parking lot for many cars that smelled of gasoline...the fragrance of industry for sure! All was gone...or was it? There in the midst of this new transformation from forest to metropolitan shopping mall and business industry was a small patch of the green emerald field left as a reminder...a memorial to the beauty of nature and in that small patch of green the little dandelion still bloomed!

Of course, no one knew of her days and nights of deep sadness, perplexing questions, upsetments and fear. Yes, she had survived, she was saved and she was still living but the little dandelion was alone. She did not feel the warmth of the surrounding cold concrete and the busy people who passed by in such a hurry (they never noticed the lonely little dandelion) so intent on a new project to make more money. Some even ate their lunch while running from one meeting to another and threw their empty sandwich paper bag on the grounds which one day gathered by the wind hit the little dandelion. She felt the bruises on her fragile and sensitive stem. Why she thought, that never happened in my home when it was the forest of harmony, care and love for one another.

The dandelion pondered her very existence and despite her shining petals she felt deep darkness. What would become of this dandelion she did not know. In fact, she worried a lot about her future and also of her new surroundings. Day in and day out no one seemed to notice the dandelion or the small patch of emerald green grass situated in the midst of this new city life. Until one day an elderly couple stopped for a visit. The little dandelion heard (with her heart of course) the couple chatting. It seemed many, many years ago (in fact well over 40) that this couple had come to the forest for a stroll and remembered the beautiful emerald green grass where they had talked of their future plans. It was here in this forest of life that the man and woman in decades past had carved their initials in a tree surrounded by a carved heart called love. It was in the forest that they shared with each other their dreams and most of all it was on the emerald green field of grass that they looked up at the clear blue sky and promised each other love forever.

Now decades later as husband and wife they returned to the forest changed. "Well honey", the elderly man said, "this place might not be our special forest anymore but it is the very ground we traveled to find and believe in God's plans for us." The woman agreed though she did voice her wish...a wish for the forest of the past back. As she said this the man said: "look, a patch of green...a sign of hope not lost!" The woman knelt down and felt the softness of the patch of green grass and with a tear of memories past she watered its very existence.

The past she realized was the gift that gave hope for newness of life. Just before they left...the couple looked back at the little patch of green. It was then that the man noticed the little dandelion standing so eloquently and resiliently amidst the concrete world built all around it. He went over and said: "Honey wait! I have a gift of love for you." And so, he handed her the precious dandelion. "Take this dandelion" he said, "this beautiful bright flower (it was never called a weed) as a reminder of my love for you forever."

The woman took the dandelion and gave her husband a hug. She held onto the dandelion all day...so tightly that the dandelion felt a bit choked up with emotion and gasping for air at times...needing the soil of earth to live. Where am I going the dandelion wondered? What is to become of me? Oh, have I any meaning left in life?

That night when the couple got home the dandelion was to listen to their reminiscing about the beautiful forest they once knew and deeply appreciated, loved and respected in their hearts and spirits. (Somehow the dandelion now knew...the forest would live on in their memory). It was then that the dandelion realized that memories are good, holy and helpful ways of treasuring life even when parts of the memories are changed, transplanted or taken away. Now the dandelion did not even have the concrete buildings as companions…and gone forever was her emerald blanket of grass that had been her trusted security where she had peacefully rested her heart and spirit.

Late that evening the woman went into her cozy kitchen to put the lights out. Just before she did that she came over to the little dandelion that she had put into a tall glass of water. She gently touched the dandelion's drooping yellow petals that had wilted during the day's journey in her hand.

She took the dandelion out of the glass of water and her own tears fell upon the petal. She whispered to the little flower (never called a weed) words of gratitude and love (we need to love all of creation) for being a reminder of her love's early years. "Oh" she said, "how blessed I am to have found you. Now I know I have a part of my forest of love, to save forever in my special book of memories. I shall press you on one of the pages."

(At first this frightened the dandelion…was she now to be crushed in spirit!?) As the woman said this, she opened up a beautiful book filled with many memories…cards, announcements of weddings, births and engagements. "Here is the page for you, my dear little dandelion. It is a page called treasure. I treasure you…you enabled me to realize today that no matter what changes come into our lives…there will always be a ray of God's sunlight. I saw and felt that today; there you were in the midst of the city bustling all around you…a shining light of sunshine, hope and renewal of spirit. Now you can live on in my heart as a reminder to treasure each moment, every relationship and most of all our love for one another and our world of creation."

Slowly and gently the woman placed the little dandelion on the precious page of her treasured memory book. She put saran wrap over the dandelion so its' fragile stem and wilted petals would not be crushed but protected and gently held as memories of joy and love. As she closed the book, the little dandelion did not feel disappointed, displaced or fearful any longer. The little dandelion had a flicker of her yellow petal still intact...she felt deep thankfulness and joy at knowing it was not being crushed but rather <u>treasured</u>. Its sunlight had served a purpose and found wonderful meaning...to remind others of God's ever abiding presence in all of life is truly a <u>holy treasure</u>.

<u>An extra thought to treasure</u>

Each day...after being placed in the book of treasures the woman would open the book up to her special page where the little dandelion with its flickering yellow petal rested. The woman would gently touch the flower (never called a weed) and whisper: "You are a reminder of love to me...I will <u>treasure</u> you forever."

What a wonderful gift we have to share with each other...the treasure of our love. No matter how fragile, displaced or weary our spirits can get...the gift of God's love can lift us up on wings of prayer and joy-filled hope and enable us to look beyond the materialism and consumerism of our world...to the very heart of our existence to share a simple light of love, to be a petal of bright compassion and a splendid root to hold us close to life's true meaning...to love one another with harmony, peace, and justice for all.

What a treasure...to see in a tiny little dandelion...the goodness of God and the reflection of Jesus' love in all of life.

(Sr. Ave Clark, O.P.)

The Little Dandelion...Treasured Forever Parable

"You are the world's light...don't hide
your light. Let it shine for all;
Let your goodness within glow for all."
(Matthew 5:13-16)

Heart-Reflection Questions:

What do you treasure in life?

Have you ever been up-rooted? How did you feel?

What do you hold most dear to your heart...as you
dare to set your heart not on worldly things?

Write your own Heart-Reflection:

Arthur's Prayer:

Let us touch one another with tenderness and reverence. Let us share compassion and hope especially
during times of trial and loss. Let us with hearts
afire, love the Lord by serving one another with humility and a grace-filled heart that says....
"I love you forever...you are a treasure... gift of God.
Amen."

The Heart

In scripture, the word "**Heart**" is mentioned over one thousand times. How fortunate we are to have a gift called <u>Heart</u> that is given many opportunities every day to share:

compassion and solace

hope and courage

forgiveness and reconciliation'

love and respect

It will be our hearts that touch pain, misfortune, or loss. It will be our hearts that embrace wounds, tragedies, and grief. It will be our hearts that **dance** with joy when healing and acceptance of life's changes or transitions unfold into a beautiful mosaic of one's own personal parable.

Arthur's heart can be described in one word – **goodness**. Goodness always tends to spread peace, mercy, and loving compassion. Arthur's heart urges us on...to become more of Jesus's love. I think of all the phone conversations with him and our visits, sitting quietly at a prayer garden, and stopping at Dunkin Donuts. I remember how happy I was to call Arthur a dear <u>heart</u> friend. I truly believe his heart and grace will continue to inspire me, and others, to be sincere and authentic in word, deed, and action.

I remember one day Arthur and I were sitting on a bench looking at the grass. He told me that the grass was <u>very green</u>! I asked him what <u>very green</u> meant. Arthur said that green was the color of hope and because I was visiting him today, he felt the grass reminded him of <u>Wonderful Hope</u>...a Hope that made him feel good about himself. He said, "that's what friendship does", and then he smiled at me. I remember smiling back and thinking, "Arthur, your friendship is like the very green grass...full of a hope that is ever so sincere and gentle. "

I feel so blessed to call Arthur my heart-friend. I hope in the reading of this book that you too have met the heart of Arthur...it is a heart that speaks with a voice of gentleness. It is a heart that sees the ordinary **very green grass** as Hope in the midst of the confusion and pressures of our modern day living. Arthur always saw a <u>patch of green Hope</u> in his daily living. In any event or encounter, he found something positive or a better way of looking at life.

Arthur knew life wasn't always fair, even to those with a **good heart.** He knew there are some things in life that one cannot change. What can be changed is one's attitude...and even one's heart. Arthur's heart always found **patches of green** ...patches of Hope even in difficult times.

I remember when in 2012 Hurricane Sandy came to the Rockaway Peninsula in New York where Arthur lived. Everyone had to be evacuated and sent to a shelter with few belongings going with them.

Arthur was just happy to <u>get a bed.</u> He never complained. I think of Arthur surviving and thriving where some people would give up, not care, and plunge into despair. He had gratitude for that bed in a shelter with very little privacy. Somehow his patch of **Green Hope** nurtured his spirit especially in times of turmoil, loss, and ordinary annoyances.

After any storm in life Arthur went through – be it physical or emotional – he was like a sunflower – or maybe even a little **golden dandelion**. He appeared **taller in spirit** with brightness that was not blinding, but rather so **welcoming.** I hope each one of us will tend to **patches of green** hope in our life and believe as Arthur did that with a heart of goodness and kindness, one can become more loving, compassionate, and accepting of our own limitations and those of others.

This is the challenge facing our very human community ~~ to <u>always</u> have hope. To see possibilities of new wholeness – to truly believe that peace will take root in the smallest patch of green. My stories and reflections on Arthur's life are less about the loss, confusion, and brokenness he experienced because of schizophrenia, but more about the power of the heart's connections to his Faithfulness of Spirit that transformed him into a treasure where Jesus' love would blossom because he stirred the patches of **ordinary graces**. To smile at a blade of grass and say, "Thank you for being Jesus' love" is an example of the heart of goodness Arthur gave to this world.

"For where your treasure is, there also will your heart be".
(Matthew 6:21)

Little Things

Two associate members of my Dominican community, Kathy and Mary, wanted to meet Arthur. Just before Christmas two years ago, they came with me to share an "indoor picnic lunch" at Arthur's residence. As Arthur entered the room where we were waiting, he asked me which lady was Mary and which one was Kathy. When I told him, he handed each one a card that said "Merry Christmas". Both women were very touched by Arthur's thoughtfulness.

Little things make a difference: holding a door, making a cup of coffee, giving a card to new friends, tying shoelaces for a man with schizophrenia, or pausing to smile at a stranger. Very often these little things we do are so easily forgotten until someone says, "Thank you for being Jesus' love." Then we are deeply moved and a sense of quiet gratitude pervades. How long will this feeling last? I hope forever. Every action, word, and deed is a wonderful gift to share with someone – a friend, a neighbor, a family member, or even a stranger.

Little things, small deeds given with a smile (Arthur always had a smile) and a sense of compassion and gentle caring, not only warm another human heart, but they can change or reconnect a spirit, console a heart loss, and bond us as companions on life's journey. These small things, small kindnesses won't take away a disease or even a sadness. What do they do? Arthur once told me that just being able to receive someone's respect and caring friendship made his day a happy one despite any struggles he was having.

This led me to think how every day each one of us gets an opportunity to give a nod, a wave, a "have a good day" to people we meet on the street, in the post office, driving on a busy highway -- really anywhere! Ordinary words, ordinary actions can become a heart to heart connection. We are all here not to ignore, diminish, or harm one another. Rather we are here to love each other into life, <u>unconditionally</u> and <u>respectfully</u>, <u>always accepting others</u> and being <u>joy-filled</u> for and with one another.

These are the actions of peace Arthur shared and lived every day. I believe he is a modern-day prophet – a prophet whose garment threads were weaved with magnificent kindness. I hope as you read this book, you too will hold the thread of Arthur's kindness and weave it into your daily life.

The smallest moments in life are the real blessings. They call us to be less selfish and to embrace the deep meaning of being grateful. When we learn to smell green grass, see the stars and enjoy the soaring birds, then we have arrived at a sacred place of sharing humanity's simplicity and nobility of life.

The Holy Spirit

Touched by the Spirit…

    the wonderful gift of the Spirit

        is **Presence.**

The very breath of God dwells in our deeds, our actions and our caring about others.

The Spirit of love knows no bounds~~

        brokenness

        wounds

        fragility of spirit

        fragmentation

        disability impairments

        physical discomforts

        mental limitations

        emotional disorder

All are held in a vessel of compassionate unity. No one is at the margins of Jesus' love ~~ all are at the center.

We live in a world that judges harshly, leaving people out (feeling rejected or forgotten). This is not living the life of the Spirit.

Many years ago, I taught students with special needs. How I loved those years! My students became my teachers ~~ they taught me to have:

peace	understanding
patience	kindness
forgiveness	compassion
sensitivity	trust
respect	concern
joy	freedom
hope	heart-prayers
simplicity	**love**

I had a sign in my classroom that said:

"Label Jars ~~Not People".

I would point to this sign every day and my students would clap so happily.

I told Arthur about that sign – he smiled and said he would have clapped too. Then he looked at me and said, "Thank you for being <u>my friend</u>". Arthur was letting me know <u>friends</u> accept one another <u>as they</u> are. When we accept one another, we are <u>giving life</u>...we are Spirit friends.

The glow of the Spirit will be seen in how we speak to or about another; how we treat one another; how we bond with each other ~~no differences separate us; rather they enhance our lives. We learn to treasure differences and see them as inspirations of acceptance.

Differences, even wounds or brokenness of spirit need not be feared or rejected. They can become a deep spiritual source of wisdom.

I found this in Arthur's life and his sharing's of how he dealt with loss, sorrow, hurts, disappointments and diminishing health.

I truly believe Arthur was <u>blessed</u> by the Spirit with an extraordinary prayer life. His relationship to Jesus was simple, sincere, honest, holy, peace filled and happy. Yes, happy! Arthur loved to pray, go to church to hear singing and praise and to find the solace of Jesus' love in his gratitude and faithfulness.

One day Arthur came to visit me. I picked him up but before we went to my home I said, "Arthur, let's stop at the shoe store". He said, "Oh Sister, you don't have to do that". I explained that friends in the prayer group wanted to share their love with him…I showed him the envelope with the money for new shoes (which he really needed!). "Well", he said, "this is a day full of the Holy Spirit. Tell the people who shared that I love them". That's the Spirit … love for sharing.

In return those who heard how happy Arthur was with his new shoes felt the <u>Spirit</u> of Arthur's loving gratitude.

You Are My Sunshine

When my mother was in an assisted living residence, I would visit her and bring my little Yorkie…his name is Mr. Sunshine. How my mom loved to put him on the seat of her walker and take him to visit all the residents, especially those who were more disabled than she. We would sing the song:

You Are My Sunshine

You are my Sunshine

My only Sunshine

You make me happy

When skies are gray

You'll never know dear

How much I love you

Please don't take

My Sunshine away!

My little Yorkie would have sort of a Yorkish grin on his face and this would make the residents feel so happy. I told Arthur the story…he said, "little animals have such joy and don't have to do much to bring happiness ~~ just be who they are".

Arthur told me he had a dog named Rusty. One day the dog was missing. He looked and looked for days. He thought his dog was gone forever. The police called a few weeks later and said they found a dog that looked like the one Arthur's family reported missing. Well…reporters took a picture of Arthur hugging his beloved dog Rusty and it was in the evening news paper! I put that clipping of a young boy named Arthur hugging his doggie next to Arthur's casket in the funeral home.

The picture said it all ~~ that doggie just looked at Arthur as he was hugged. Yes …a picture of sunshine…joy, love and happiness…a picture of being a young child hugging a lost doggie.

Arthur told me he never forgot how he felt when his doggie was lost. He wondered if he could ever be happy again.

We all have had moments in life of different losses at different ages~~and we wondered...how will we be happy again? What ray of sunshine will encourage us to get up...believe...and not lose hope?

"Arthur", I asked, "What did finding the lost dog mean to you?" He told me that he felt whatever would happen in life, he would always remember the moment of his doggie being returned...he felt that moment could be stirred into other experiences. I said, "You sure have done that Arthur". All his losses, his diminishing health, and his struggles...would never take from Arthur the memory of feeling the sun-shine in his heart.

So often we learn a lesson, feel a reprieve of suffering, have some comfort and hope ... what do we do with these wonderful grace-filled moments when life changes? Forget them, feel lost or defeated again? Let's do what Arthur did ~~ stir the memory, stir the <u>presence</u> of a hope that always has energy, that is renewable and life sustaining. Stir the memory of the sunshine of Jesus' forever love…always there.

Life Is a Blessing

One of the happiest days of Arthur's life was the day he became a Catholic. He told me he felt so close to Jesus on that day. Arthur loved Jesus' way of living and being for others. Arthur sincerely believed that Jesus was always there for him. "Come follow me" ...this is what Arthur did in his everyday life. The very way Arthur would look at someone was always with respect and genuine kindness. His gaze was the gaze of Jesus' love.

Anyone who knew Arthur felt that his goodness and kindness were reflections of Jesus' love. Arthur's way of life was, I believe, rooted in the Beatitudes ~~ in the blessedness of giving to others the mercy and compassion of Jesus' love and forgiveness, encouragement and companionship.

Despite any setbacks or difficulties Arthur would have in life, he always had a positive and sensible way of looking at and dealing with life's zigs-zags and detours. What always came across in these times of heartache and loss would be Arthur's trust and positive attitude...believing in the graces of better possibilities and options to choose from to renew his spirit.

In one incident in particular, I asked Arthur, "What will you do?" ... his wallet was lost and when found, many of his treasured pictures and holy cards had been taken or tossed on the sidewalk. He told me he was grateful for what was found and never lamented all that was lost ... and never mentioned the money in the wallet that was gone. He focused on what was found and told me he forgave whoever took the things from his wallet.

Perhaps the blessing of Arthur's example lies in the fact that he did not harbor any harsh feelings. He told me that every day when he would get up he would look out his window and thank God for another

day … and then he would add … to do good in Jesus
name. Arthur had found the peace of becoming the person he was meant to be.

This is what a person like Arthur saw in living the Beatitudes:

B~   best word is Love

E~   extra caring

A~   adapt to life

T~   touch of Love

I~   invited others to be friends

T~   time for compassion

U~   understanding heart

D~   devoted to Jesus Love

E~   example lived

S~   sharing the Gospel

Arthur's faith from the day he processed down the church aisle with his sponsor, Celeste, by his side to become a Catholic...would be a forever sacred moment of happiness...a moment of truly uniting his life journey with Jesus. Arthur was, and will always be an example to all those who knew him...an example of what it means, not just to see life as a blessing, but to become a blessing of Jesus' love in the world.

Hidden Graces

We hear stories of people doing things they never thought they would – a man jumping off a subway platform to save a stranger from an oncoming train barely escapes to safety. What inner spark of the human spirit moved that man to help someone he did not know and put himself in danger?! It was the inner spirit of goodness. We all have it ... stir the flame of your inner goodness every day and you will see a new creation in our world.

Arthur and I discussed the story of the man saving the life of a stranger. Arthur felt the man had a holy heart...he forgot himself so he could save another person.

"How do you forget yourself, Arthur," I asked. "Well", he said, "sometimes I am very tired and weary and someone knocks on my door. I think to myself, how would I feel if no one answered or the per-

son pretended they were asleep or yelled 'go away'.
So, I answer my door and enjoy chatting or even
just listening or lending the person $3.00".

There it is...the hidden grace <u>not to count the</u>
<u>cost</u>...to take time **to be** presence to another human
being.

There is an inspiring piece of art by Cindy McKenna
picturing Christ walking on the water holding a heart
going towards a boat. There are beautiful colorful
bubbles of light showing Christ on the way to the
boat. Christ is looking lovingly at the heart. Somehow this picture reminds me of Arthur. At times Arthur has been the heart held by Christ bringing him
to the safety of the boat. At other times, I see Arthur
as Christ's love carrying the heart of another to safety. The title given to the art piece is "Take Courage".
I think that is a good title and the way in which each
of us can take courage is to believe in the hidden
graces of our own goodness.

Thirteen years ago, I was hit by a runaway 12-ton locomotive train. No one was on it ~~ it rolled down a hill, picked up speed and slowed down only when it crashed into any car in its path. My car was hit and I ended up with severe injuries that required surgeries, rehab, and a will to live … to get up again and walk with pain. My inner graces were stirred by others' compassion and care but I had to **take courage** and believe I'd walk despite any pain… and I continue to do so.

Arthur sent me a card that said:
> "Get Well Sister, I feel your pain. I believe
> you 'll walk – just lean on Jesus' love"

I never forgot Arthur's card and I still lean on Jesus' love. I told Arthur once how much his card meant to me. He said," "Sister, I knew you could do it because you see Jesus in everybody, even me." "Arthur", I said, "you were one of my special hidden graces that kept me going." He smiled and said, "isn't it great

185

when we realize we all get a chance to lean on Jesus' love in one another."

You are so right Arthur …hmmm I thought, somehow, I will always believe Arthur is carrying Jesus merciful compassionate love for all of us…a special messenger of God's love. Arthur was a hidden grace for me. I'll never forget his humble wisdom.

Echoes of Love

When I was six years old, my dad took me to the top of a mountain. Once there, we would shout out some words. I was so surprised to hear a girl's voice coming from the other side of the mountain that sounded just like me and said the same things I did. When my dad told me that it was my voice I said, "But dad, that voice is coming from over the river." He laughed and explained that it was an ECHO!

As the years passed my dad would retell the echo story but in a new way. He would tell me that goodness and kindness and good deeds could be an ECHO. What we say...how we say it...what we do...how we do it ... all can have an ECHO effect on others. If we have an open heart and kind attitude, it will become a great noble ECHO of love for our world. If we are harsh, judgmental, or unforgiving, then the echo becomes a negative, self-defeating one that is devoid of life-giving ways.

There was never unkindness in any of Arthur's words. I never heard gossip or words that would diminish anyone's life. In fact, Arthur used words that were always uplifting, hope-filled and very caring. How did Arthur live that way? It is so easy to get annoyed even with small things. We end up magnifying some misdeed or hurtful words others say to us. Arthur saw a better way...it would be the way of Jesus. "Love one another as I have loved you". **Forgive 70 x 70!** "Love is patient, kind, not jealous..." (1Cor. 13:4)

Arthur did not just read the Gospel or hear the words of scripture proclaimed. He let the words become part of him...Arthur became the word of Jesus' love through his kindness, patience and acceptance of others. He did not have a pulpit or stage to proclaim what he believed in...Arthur had something better-- a connection to human hearts. People were changed just by being with him.

Arthur told me once when he was taking a walk he saw a man at a bus stop fumbling through his bag…apparently looking for his bus card. As he got closer, Arthur asked the man if he needed a card. When the man said yes, Arthur gave him his card. "What will you do now?" the man asked. Arthur replied, "I'll be happy that you were able to get on the bus you were waiting for." The man took the card, gave Arthur a hug and said, "Sir, you are a fine gentleman and I will never forget your kindness." Arthur watched as the man got on the bus and they waved to each other as if they were forever friends. I asked Arthur what he did then and he said, "I took a long walk and felt so good inside."

This story could be a parable about a modern **Good Samaritan** "doing unto others as we would like it done to us", or perhaps it is just a very inspiring story of how we all are called to love, and in giving we will receive far more.

Just imagine how happy Arthur felt as the man waved with such joy. This can be our joy too!

In giving -- we become LOVE

In giving --one should not look for what it
            does for us

In giving -- not from our abundance, but all
            from the heart

In giving -- we are creating a world-order of
            sharing, not hoarding

In giving -- we might not ever know the fruits
            of our gift…it does not matter

In giving -- we become the glory of Jesus love
            here on earth.

Thoughts and Reflections

I've learned that-"no matter what happens or how
bad it seems today, life does go on
and will be better tomorrow"

I've learned that-"you can tell a lot about a person by
the way he or she handles these
three things: a rainy day, lost
luggage and tangles of Christmas
tree lights"

I've learned that-"regardless of your relationship
with your parents, you'll miss them
when they're gone from your life"

I've learned that-"making a living is not the same as
making a life"

I've learned that-"life sometimes gives you a second
chance"

I've learned that-"whenever I decide something with
an open heart, I usually make the
right decision"

I've learned that-"every day you should reach out
and touch someone. People love a
warm hug or just a friendly at on
the back"

I've learned that-"even when I have pains, I don't
have to be one"
I've learned that-"I still have a lot to learn"
I've learned that-"people will forget what you said,
people will forget what you did, but
people will never forget how you
made them feel" (Maya Angelou)

Arthur loved these thoughts by Maya Angelou. We
would discuss them during some of our phone conversations. Arthur added another **I've learned:**
I've learned -   "to always remember how Jesus
made me feel...special, holy, and
being a messenger of his love in my
own way" (Arthur Mirell)

"The gift of life
God's special gift
is no less beautiful when
it is accompanied by
illness or weakness,
hunger or poverty,
mental or physical handicaps,
loneliness or old age.
Indeed, at these times
human life gains
extra splendor
as it requires our special care,
concern and reverence.
It is in and through
the weakest
human vessels that the Word
continues to reveal
the power of His love."

(Terrance Cardinal Cooke)

Arthur was very touched by Cardinal Cooke's words. He told me it made him feel <u>honored</u> and <u>blessed</u> to be a human vessel that reveals the power of Jesus' love. I asked Arthur how he does this and he reverently answered – "I ask God to use me as he wishes".

<u>Song of Hope</u>

My song of Hope is born
      in compassion embraced
My song of Hope is born
      in scars blessed
My song of Hope is born
      in gratitude for Arthur's love and
      sincerity
My song of Hope is born
      in love and peace
My song of Hope is born
      upon the cross of Christ's love.

(Sister Ave Clark, O.P.)

Advice From A Pot

Be Well-Rounded

   Keep In Shape

      Hold Your Own

         Don't Go To Pieces

         Serve Others

            Chip In When You Need To

               Get All Fired Up! (Your True Nature)

Arthur and I had a good laugh about the Pot story. He said, "Sister, I love that last line – Get All Fired Up. I do that when I pray." Amen

"Arthur lived through examples, rather than power"

                    (a friend from Church)

"I don't think Arthur is resting in peace but rather Risen in Glory!"   (a friend from Church)

Remembering Arthur

I asked some friends who knew Arthur if they would write something about how he had touched their life or how they would describe him.   As you read these reflections I think you will smile and feel that you now know this good man and can say, "thank you for being Jesus' Love."

I had the honor of knowing Arthur. I remember when he first wanted to become a Catholic. We spent time together talking about the Catholic faith. It was a joy when he was baptized. Arthur was happy to be a Catholic He truly was a child of God. I thank the community at St. Jude's for accepting him and making him feel welcome.
(Father Mike Tedone)

Arthur was kind, holy and gentle.
(Kathy Sheridan)

Arthur Mirell was a dear friend to my husband Pete and I. His faith in Jesus was an inspiration and he was a man of great patience. He endued much suffering without com-plaint. He had a loving heart and to us he was a "gentle giant" in so many ways.

(Nina and (Pete from Heaven) Siggia)

Psalm 32:2 "Happy the man…in whose spirit there is no guile"

These words for me personify Arthur Mirell. We met three years ago through our mutual friend, Sister Ave Clark, O.P. Since then we shared celebrating life and sharing our lives with Arthur in all its' ups and downs with meals, prayers, songs and words of encouragement.

I share with you what he wrote in one of his cards to me:

To Mary, "May Jesus always love you in His heart like Sister Ave's Heart to Heart Ministry loves everybody.

Arthur

Arthur will always remind me on so many different levels of God's love.

(Mary Morris)

Arthur was so very proud to wear his baptismal robe at the Easter Vigil. He stood so tall and sure of himself as he walked to the Baptismal Font. His face was very focused and his eyes reflected the flowing waters of new life! When my family and I drove him home after the Easter Vigil, Arthur said to us: "thank you for being a good Catholic family"

I was honored to be his sponsor and my heart was so enriched by Arthur's faith.

(Celeste Grillo)

I remember Arthur saying over and over again: "the best thing I ever did was become a Catholic."

The last card I received from Arthur was remembering the Holy Thursday when I washed his feet a few years ago. What a profound grace that was for me to wash Arthur's feet.

(Sister Mary Steifvater)

Arthur Mirell lived a remarkable life. Born to Jewish par-
ents, his knowledge of Judaism and becoming a Catholic
through the RCIA Program at the Shrine of St. Jude in
Brooklyn, NY enriched his knowledge of the Scriptures.
Christianity was projected through his sincere and simple
thoughtful ways. His favorite prayer time was at the First
Friday all night prayer vigil to the Sacred Heart at the
chapel with the Apostleship of Prayer group.
Arthur had a pretty good memory. He remembered birth-
days and sent cards. What really touched me with the
practice of his faith is the fact that he was a true witness to
the Messianic prophecy: "But a shoot shall sprout from
the stump of Jesse and from its' roots a bud shall blossom."
Isaiah 11:1
Arthur came to know Jesus Christ~~the Messiah.
Arthur, I shall always remember you. It is an honor to
memorialize Arthur and his great faith.
(Terry Refol)

We came to know Arthur because we belong to the same parish. Aside from seeing Arthur in church every Sunday, he also attended almost all the activities of the church both social and spiritual. After receiving his sacraments through the RCIA program, he joined church organizations like the Apostleship of Prayer and the Holy Name Society to which we also belong.

Because of this, we came to know him even more. He was such an inspiration because despite his problems with schizophrenia and being the only Catholic in his Jewish family, he demonstrated a very good understanding of the Catholic faith…and he lived it too!

He was always present during our First Friday Holy Family prayer hour and overnight adoration of the Blessed Sacrament and in every Holy Name Society meeting and activities.

On a personal note, he was so loving and caring, always interested to know how we were and the whole family, not only when we say him in person but also he called our home just to ask how we were doing even after he moved out of the community. Arthur left us this legacy of being able to live the faith and being so faithful to God even in the presence of health issues and disabilities. He will always be an inspiration to us.

(Rudy and Tessie Sugarte)

The first time I heard about a man named Arthur was through Sister Ave Clark, O.P. on her visits to St. Jude's parish. Sister would always have a fascinating story about this man; his family, his phone calls to her, things that they did together, or sometimes a problem that he may have been having at the time. Whatever the story was, it always had my attention. I wondered just who is this man named Arthur?

My curiosity about Arthur was about to be lessened. Sister Ave was having a birthday celebration for Arthur and I was invited. Eager to know this person that

Sister Ave had always spoke so highly of, I could not wait for the party.

The day had come, and I arrived at the party to finally meet him. Arthur definitely lived up to everything Sister Ave had said about him. He had a marvelous presence, and I found that he also had a gentleness about him that drew people to him. Arthur spoke to everyone at the party, including me and told numerous stories about his family and many other intriguing things. I had made a new friend.

Arthur was not a well man; he suffered with an illness that ultimately led him to God. I am saddened that our friendship had ended in such a short time. I am a better person for knowing Arthur. He was a generous soul, always giving to others when he was in need himself. Arthur was so kind and loving even when he was hurt by others. He was inspirational and in my heart, I believe that he tried to live like Jesus and follow a path of love. Forever my friend.

(MaryAnn Delgardio)

Epilogue

I hope as you read the chapters and stories about Arthur's life that you felt the wonderful inspiration of such a fine person. Perhaps you might even feel gratitude for the way in which Arthur so courageously lived his life; always thinking of others and forging peace by being a person of deep forgiveness, compassion and love. Arthur was an ambassador of Jesus' reconciliation and hope to and with everyone he met, especially those with special needs. His unshakeable Faith informed his worldly gestures of acceptance, kindness and heartfelt mercy.

Arthur believed that the greatness of meaning in life lies in how we put the Gospel at the center of our being. Arthur for sure lived a life of spiritual depth and meaning. I believe we all can learn from his life how to share hope, trust in God, and believe that there are no limits to love.

Pope Francis once said, "Hope is the virtue of a heart that doesn't dwell on the past, but is able to see a tomorrow." Arthur was such a heart...a heart that was humble in spirit and a heart that embraced everyone. Arthur truly became the heart of Jesus' Love by sharing the spirit of the Gospel message...

"love one another as I have loved you."

What else can I say except so deeply
from my heart...
Thank you, Arthur, for being Jesus' Love!

Acknowledgements

I would like to thank Arthur for inspiring me to write this book about him. His goodness and kindness can now be remembered by all those people who read it.

To my dear and caring friend, Peg Franco, who encouraged me to write this book when it was only a hope-wish in my heart. Peg did the first typing and reading of my handwriting and notes scribbled in the margins.

I especially want to thank Susan Schwemmer...my dedicated typist and editor and late-night email sender of chapters for me to read, review and re-write. Her son, Eric, great on the computer, was able to navigate us to sites and help us get to the finished product. To Mary Morris, Kathy Sheridan and Judy Tolan for doing the final editing and suggestions for the placement of book chapters.

To these wonderful friends I cannot thank you enough. You labored heart to heart and I truly believe you were <u>blessed</u> to be the first people to read Arthur's words and appreciate his extraordinary courage that shaped his wonderful faith-life. I say to each of you as Arthur would:

<u>Thank you for being Jesus' Love!</u>

Sister Ave Clark, O.P., is an Amityville, New York Dominican Sister. She co-ordinates Heart to Heart Ministry. Sister is a retreat presenter and a certified pastoral counselor. She also treasures Arthur's friendship as a wonderful blessing in her life.

Thank You for Being Jesus' Love